TODAY
IN MY GARDEN

365 Tips for Your
Northwest Garden

Foreword by Mary Robson

Cool Springs Press
Franklin, Tennessee

Published by Cool Springs Press, 101 Forrest Crossing Boulevard,
Franklin, Tennessee 37064

Dunn, Teri. Today in my garden : 365 tips for your Northwest garden /
Teri Dunn; foreword by Mary Robson.
p. cm.
ISBN-10: 1-59186-341-4 (pbk.)
ISBN-13: 978-1-59186-341-0
1. Gardening—Northwestern States. I. Title. II.
Title: 365 tips for your Northwest garden.
SB451.34.N96D86 2006
635.0975—dc22
2006028093

First Printing: 2006
Printed in Canada
10 9 8 7 6 5 4 3 2 1

Visit the Cool Springs Press website at www.coolspringspress.net.

Never leave that
till tomorrow which
you can do today.

—*Ben Franklin*

CONTENTS

FOREWORD

APPENDIX

❧ EVERYDAY TIP ❧

Get into the habit of keeping a garden journal. It's like a "baby album" for your garden. It is invaluable for jotting down notes about problems or successes, storing articles from newspapers or magazines, or attaching photos. It doesn't have to be fancy, but spiral binding, tabbed pages, and pockets are convenient. (It makes a great gift, too!)

FOREWORD

Gardening brings us close to life, giving us the joy of touching warm earth, rejoicing in rain that reaches plant roots, and allowing us to harvest fresh foods and bountiful flowers.

For many of us, the treasured moments in our gardens come as we walk slowly—perhaps with a cup of

tea or coffee in hand—to observe the
daily changes in the buds, seeds, fruit,
and flowers. Change brings fascination
in every season.

Sometimes the garden baffles us:
What needs to be done next? Can you
transplant, start seeds, prune? This
collection of 365 tips for your Northwest garden helps focus on seasonally
appropriate activities, to guide you in

the planning of tasks to support and
improve your garden day by day.

WHERE ARE YOU IN THE NORTHWEST

The beautiful Northwest—here defined
as including Idaho, northern California,
Oregon, and Washington—ranges from
Pacific Ocean edges to the mountains
of the Cascades, Olympics, and Rockies.

Ocean influences bring maritime mildness to regions west of the Cascade Mountains; while altitude and interior weather influences increase winter cold and summer heat east of the Cascades. You'll get the most help from this book by first checking your own zone and weather conditions year-round. Spring's arrival varies from south to north: what's happening

in northern California may be 6 to
8 weeks earlier than growth in Idaho.

Climate ranges from USDA zone
3 in Idaho to USDA zone 9 along
the southern Oregon and northern
California coasts also mean that plants
hardy in one part of the region may be
less so in colder sections. Your local
nurseries and garden experts will help
you with plant choice specifics.

Rainfall. Though our region differs considerably in winter low temperatures, all parts of it share one reality: summer rain is scarce. Moisture falls in winter and early spring as rain or snow but lessens drastically from June through September. Rain declines just when plants begin active growth and require water. You'll find tips for using soaker hoses to supply necessary moisture in the most efficient way.

Soils. Northwestern soils vary as much as do Northwestern temperatures. Along the Pacific coast, influences from ancient glaciers have left gravelly, rocky, often acidic soils with little organic content. River valleys like the Willamette Valley in Oregon have enviably deep, workable soils. Soils east of the Cascades may be alkaline, or may contain deep deposits of mineral-laden dust from ancient and modern volcanic eruptions such as Mount St. Helens in 1980.

All these soils, whatever the type in your particular region, will benefit from regular applications of coarse organic mulch to help control weeds and hold in scarce moisture.

Enjoy Your Daily Observations

Traveling through the garden will be enhanced by keeping a simple journal; but, don't make your notes more complicated than you need. Allow them to carry the smear of mud or the pressed plant that's part of your daily observations.

Using tips from this book can also help you learn from your garden, by looking for the connection between the suggestions and what's moving about in your own world.

Enjoy the daily, weekly, and yearly progress of your garden and your own increased knowledge about it. Just as you enrich the soil of your garden, your garden will enrich your life.

—*Mary Robson*

❖ SPRING ❖

❧ EVERYDAY TIP ❧

If you haven't already
done so, sketch a map of your
garden (it can be simple!)
noting the areas that receive full
sun, a mix of sun and shade,
or full shade. Knowing this is
invaluable to selecting the right
plant, for the right spot.

❧ TIP I ❧

Fill a windowbox. First make
sure any remnants of last year's show
have been scraped out. Put in
fresh potting soil. Arrange the pots of
plants atop the soil first, and
shift them around if you wish—sort
of a dress rehearsal. Then plant them
at the level they were in the pot, and
water everything thoroughly.

☐ *Check when completed*

❖ TIP 2 ❖

Buy a watering wand. It attaches to the end of a hose and delivers a softer, soaking spray that is ideal for watering seedlings and new transplants without knocking them over. Look for one that has a handy thumb-operated on-off valve. Some models have several settings, so you can choose from mist, gentle shower, or jet spray.

☐ *Check when completed*

❧ TIP 3 ❧

You'll likely notice that your house-plants are starting to show new growth. This is a response not just to milder weather but longer day length. So go ahead and give them more water and ramp up a regular fertilizing regimen. If they grow too vigorously for their assigned space, pinch back the tips to encourage more compact, bushier plants.

☐ *Check when completed*

❧ TIP 4 ❧

Start seeds of warm-season veggies—such as tomatoes, peppers, eggplant, and squash—indoors. Get everything off to a good start with a nice, gentle soaking. Provide good indoor brightness by using fluorescent lights or grow lights.

❏ *Check when completed*

❧ TIP 5 ❧

Feed your roses after they
begin leafing out and flower buds
show a bit of color. Special fertilizers
are sold for roses, but you can also
use an all-purpose formulation.
Deliver the fertilizer with plenty of
water so it all soaks in.

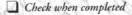 *Check when completed*

❧ TIP 6 ❧

When watering shrubs, rosebushes, and trees, a slow, deep soaking is much better than occasional lighter sprinklings. Set the hose (or a soaker hose) at the base of the plant, at a slow trickle, and come back in an hour or so. Check with a trowel to see whether moisture has penetrated to the roots. If not, repeat as needed.

☐ *Check when completed*

❧ TIP 7 ❧

Don't rush vegetable plantings
for warm-weather crops—the seeds
languish or even rot in cold,
damp ground. Wait until the soil
warms. It's fine to plant spinach,
lettuce, peas, and onions now.
Always sow more than you think
you'll need; you can thin later.

☐ *Check when completed*

❧ TIP 8 ❧

Prune frost-damaged plants
back to live wood. Healthy wood is
tinged with green under the bark
and has white pith. But wait a bit if
the plant seems dead—they can
revive as late as June.

☐ *Check when completed*

❖ TIP 9 ❖

This time of year, if you're walking around in flowerbeds or the vegetable garden, tidying up and making plans, you should be careful. Partially frozen and wet soil is easily compacted or damaged by your footsteps. Lay down some planks to walk on; these redistribute your weight more evenly.

☐ *Check when completed*

❖ TIP 10 ❖

To get a fabulous performance out of your camellias and rhododendrons, feed them just as growth begins. Both types of plants prefer soil on the acidic side. If your soil is not acidic, or not enough, the right fertilizer will do the trick. Apply it at the rates recommended on the label.

☐ *Check when completed*

❧ TIP II ❧

Till under or dig in cover crops
that you sowed earlier—as soon as
the soil is workable. This timing
will be important if you want the
plants to contribute organic matter
and texture to an area that you
will be planting in. They need time
to break down, to meld.

☐ *Check when completed*

✣ TIP 12 ✣

Plant jack-o-lantern pumpkins
now (as well as those cute little mini
pumpkins that are so handy for
decorating) if you want to harvest
by Halloween. Start the seeds
indoors in pots or flats. Cover them
with a thin coating of soil mix, and
place in a warm spot. They'll
germinate quickly.

❑ *Check when completed*

✤ TIP 13 ✤

Have the seeds you started indoors
begun to poke their heads up? When
the first true set of leaves appears
(technically the second set; the
leaves look different from the first,
lowest ones), use a small pair of
sharp scissors to thin out smaller or
weaker ones right at soil level.

☐ *Check when completed*

❖ TIP 14 ❖

Now is the time to go after
dandelions in your lawn. Mow them
down or pinch off their flowers
while they're still yellow . . . before
they have a chance to go to seed. If
there aren't too many of them,
you're best off digging them
out by their long roots, so they're
gone for good.

☐ *Check when completed*

✤ Tip 15 ✤

Violets and violas are coming into bloom. This is the only time they are adorable—later in the season, they sow all over the place. After a few years, you'll have more than you want. So try to set aside your sentimentality and pull out some of them now.

☐ *Check when completed*

❧ TIP 16 ❧

Spring is a great time to move a
shrub or small tree to a new
location, while the plant is still
dormant. Early March offers a good
chance to transplant, so the shrub or
tree can direct all its energy into a
great show when it does start
growing. Just be sure the soil is
neither frozen nor soggy.

❑ *Check when completed*

✤ TIP 17 ✤

Celebrate St. Patrick's Day
with your own green carnations!
Just buy some white ones, recut
their bases, and put them in a vase
of water to which you have added
several drops of green food coloring.
After a few hours, if the color is too
light, take out the flowers for a
moment and stir in a few more
drops of food coloring.

☐ *Check when completed*

MARCH

❖ TIP 18 ❖

Take a critical look at the
ornamental trees in your yard,
before they are lush with foliage.
They may benefit from some
judicious thinning of their interior
about now. Just don't overdo it—
this isn't even a job you'll do every
year. Take out no more than a third
of any branch at any one time;
preserve the canopy's shape.

❏ *Check when completed*

❧ TIP 19 ❧

Visit your groundcover areas and
check for invading weeds.
Springtime makes unwanted plants
grow fast, too! The good news,
however, is that it's easier to yank
them out now. Not just because
they're smaller—if it's been rainy
lately, the roots of the weeds are
much easier to extract.

☐ *Check when completed*

❦ TIP 20 ❦

Aerating can relieve an
unhealthy lawn on compacted
ground. Use a spading fork or
special spiked shoes made
for this job, or rent a hand-operated
tool. The goal, in any case, is to
punch shallow holes into the grass
at regular intervals to let in water
and air. Work right after a rain, or
water well the day before.

❏ *Check when completed*

❧ TIP 21 ❧

Decorate a lamppost! Wrap it with a
4-foot-tall, slender piece of chicken
wire, overlapping the ends and
cinching them tightly in place (use
wire cutters rather than your fingers—
it's easier on your hands). When the
weather warms, plant a climbing vine
right at the base. By midsummer,
foliage and flowers will hide the wire.

☐ *Check when completed*

❧ TIP 22 ❧

Fertilize plants in active growth,
watering before and after feeding.
Use an all-purpose garden fertilizer
for most all your plants, and
purchase special fertilizers for plants
with special needs. Whatever you
use, always apply according to
the label instructions.

❑ *Check when completed*

❖ TIP 23 ❖

Prevent damping-off disease, a
fungus that attacks developing
seedlings, causing them to shrivel
and die right at soil level. The fungi
thrive in stagnant air and high
humidity. An ounce of prevention is
worth a pound of cure, so use clean
containers and a sterile, soilless
seed-starting mix.

☐ *Check when completed*

❖ TIP 24 ❖

Check on all your developing
seedlings. Remember to water
before feeding, or at the same time,
so the roots can take up the
nutrients. If the seedlings are
leaning towards the light source,
move the trays or pots a quarter
turn each day to encourage the
stems to grow upright.

☐ *Check when completed*

❦ TIP 25 ❦

Head off lawn-mowing
challenges by displaying your
birdbath, sundial, garden bench, or
other décor up on paving blocks.
Seat the paver securely in the
ground. Don't forget to check that
it's level (this is particularly
important if you are using more
than one to support a single item).

☐ *Check when completed*

MARCH

❧ TIP 26 ❧

If you have a cold frame, or
have been thinking of making one,
early spring is a good time to
launch it. Little seedlings can be
raised and acclimated in its shelter.
Be sure to water the seedlings
in the morning so the foliage has a
chance to dry before evening.

❏ *Check when completed*

⁕ TIP 27 ⁕

Zap weeds in the cracks of your sidewalk, walkway, patio, or driveway, one by one, safely. Just fill a spray bottle with white vinegar (with a few drops of dish soap to contribute stickiness) and hit each one with a strong blast. If the weed isn't dead in a day, spray it again . . . it should succumb.

☐ *Check when completed*

❖ TIP 28 ❖

Pull weeds out by the roots.
They compete with your plants,
especially the new and smaller ones,
hogging valuable resources of soil
nutrients, water, and sunlight.
Often they harbor insects and plant
diseases, too. It is much easier to get
out the entire weed when the
ground is damp, after a rain or
shortly after you've watered.

❏ *Check when completed*

❖ TIP 29 ❖

Remove diseased, infested, or
dead leaves whenever you see them.
Don't let them just fall off and
hang around the base of your plants,
where they can harbor and
encourage problems. Get that stuff
out—way out. Don't even toss it on
your compost pile. Send it away
with the household waste pick-up.

❏ *Check when completed*

❖ TIP 30 ❖

Make patch repairs to your lawn. Rake the bare spots beforehand, and then broadcast grass seed as evenly as you can. Then top off with a thin layer of soil. Water gently with a sprinkler now, and daily until the grass has sprouted and is growing well. Fertilize after the grass has been mowed for the first time.

❏ *Check when completed*

❧ TIP 31 ❧

Now is a fine time to lay sod, which
is especially suitable for slopes.
Prepare the area by stripping away
former plantings and removing
rocks, weeds, and roots. Till lightly
to loosen the soil, sprinkle a little
lawn fertilizer (follow the amount
directions on the bag), and rake
smooth. Put the sod down on a
cool, cloudy day, and water well.

☐ *Check when completed*

❧ TIP 32 ❧

Now is also a good time to
sow new lawns using locally
available grass seed. Clear out the
planting area, add weed-free
organic matter, and rake smooth. If
you don't use a mechanical seeder,
just broadcast left to right, and then
up and down, to make sure the
whole area is covered. Keep it moist
so the seeds can germinate.

☐ *Check when completed*

❧ TIP 33 ❧

Pick out or make up a planting
area with excellent drainage, and fill
it with bulbs of summer bloomers.
Favorites include calla lily, dahlia,
and canna. Do not plant too deeply
or closely. Water the bed lightly
afterwards, and maintain even
moisture over the coming weeks to
give them a good start.

☐ *Check when completed*

❧ TIP 34 ❧

Combat pesky rabbits. Garden centers sell special "rabbit fencing," which is a bigger mesh than chicken wire. Wrap individual plants or envelop a flowerbed or the vegetable patch. Be sure to sink the fencing down into the ground by several inches, so they cannot get under it.

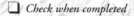 *Check when completed*

❦ TIP 35 ❦

If a deer fence is not practical
for your yard, you may have some luck
discouraging deer with repellents.
You'll find plenty of products sold for
this purpose, though they ought to be
replenished after a rain. Or suspend—
on string or twine—bars of soap from
branches. (Irish Spring and Lifebuoy
are particularly intense). Deer get used
to these; change scents often.

❑ *Check when completed*

❧ TIP 36 ❧

Create a focal-point planting. First, select a big, dramatic, or unusual pot or urn. To make it stand out further, elevate it on a support (a pedestal, overturned pot, or stack of bricks). Then fill it with enough plants so that it can be admired from any angle. Pick colors that contrast with the surroundings so it automatically captures attention.

☐ *Check when completed*

❧ TIP 37 ❧

Check on established vines as
well as ones you planted this year.
Most are surging into growth.
If you don't intervene sooner rather
than later, and direct the stems
where you want them to go, the
whole display can get out of control
pretty quickly. Train and tie
elongating branches onto their
support with strips of soft cloth.

☐ *Check when completed*

❖ TIP 38 ❖

Tall-growing perennials often benefit from staking—foxgloves, hollyhocks, verbascums, penstemons, and delphiniums, to name a few. If you didn't insert something at planting time, it's probably not too late. Just poke the support securely into the ground close by, and attach the plant to it at intervals with soft ties.

☐ *Check when completed*

❧ TIP 39 ❧

Nip insect-pest problems early.
If you don't know their identity, look
them up in a gardening book or show
a sample to someone knowledgeable
so you can learn how to fight off
infestations. When you see harmful
bugs or beetles dining on your
flowerbeds or in your vegetable
garden, handpick them and toss them
in a bucket of soapy water.

☐ *Check when completed*

❧ TIP 40 ❧

Little groundcover plants are for sale
now. But do your homework—is
your intended site sunny or shady?
Do you want something that
flowers? Then prepare the spot,
clearing it out and adding organic
matter. Don't set the plants too close
together; they will fill in. After
planting, lay down a mulch to keep
them moist and prevent weeds.

❏ *Check when completed*

❖ TIP 41 ❖

Be on the lookout for seedling
trees. They can pop up anywhere in
the yard, but are a problem where
you've put a mulch of chopped-up
fall leaves. These pests can elbow
out plants you want, while hogging
water and soil nutrients. It's tedious,
but you'd best yank them out or cut
them down with a sharp hoe.

☐ *Check when completed*

❖ TIP 42 ❖

Spread compost. Whether store-
bought or homemade, it is
always beneficial for your garden,
especially early in the season. Because
compost is sometimes still decom-
posing, it generates some heat, a
hedge against springtime's temperature swings. Sprinkle to a depth of
1 to 3 inches, broadcasting it by hand,
or with a trowel or shovel.

☐ *Check when completed*

❧ TIP 43 ❧

Plant annuals, but keep plastic
protection handy for colder nights.
Be sure to water in each one
well and to water consistently over
the coming days and weeks so
they can "get their legs under them"
and prosper. Top off the
planting area with some moisture-
retaining mulch.

☐ *Check when completed*

❧ TIP 44 ❧

A big pot need not be superheavy. Don't fill it completely with potting soil when the plants within use only a few inches' worth. Instead, put a layer of foam peanuts in the bottom first. Nobody will know, the plants will be fine, and you'll be able to pick up the pot and move it if you want.

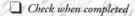 *Check when completed*

❧ TIP 45 ❧

Deadhead spent bulb flowers promptly. There's no reason to keep them; if you did, the plants would try to expend valuable energy forming seeds. Plus, removing them keeps your displays looking tidier and fresher longer. A good way to do this is to go out and pick bouquets for the house.

☐ *Check when completed*

❧ TIP 46 ❧

While perennials are still
emerging or young, you should
insert stakes or other supports. This
way, there is less risk of harming
their root systems. Another benefit
of acting now is that you can
start fastening the plants early,
saving the headache of emergency
interventions later in the season.

❏ *Check when completed*

❦ TIP 47 ❦

Once your spring-flowering shrubs
(such as rhododendrons) are
finished blooming, you may go out
and prune and shape them. Don't
wait too long; they will soon start
developing buds for next year's
show, and you don't want to trim off
those. While you're at it, do some
thinning—the plants will look
better and be healthier as a result.

☐ *Check when completed*

❧ TIP 48 ❧

Don't toss out that potted
Easter lily. It may live to bloom
again. Wait till the flowers are spent,
then clip them off (but not the
stalk). Put the pot in a sheltered
spot outside and water regularly. In
a few weeks, whenever temperatures
become steadily warm, you can
plant it in the ground.

❏ *Check when completed*

❧ TIP 49 ❧

Divide overgrown perennials, ones in large clumps, or ones that seem to be less productive every year. Discard the center of the old plant and save the outer sections— make sure each piece has a good clump of roots and some emerging green growth. Replant, evenly spaced, and water well.

☐ *Check when completed*

❖ TIP 50 ❖

Spring is a fine time to remove
a tree limb. Assuming it's not too
thick or too high up, you can
do this yourself with a good sharp
handsaw. Use the three-cuts
method: an undercut halfway up; an
overcut a bit farther out and halfway
down (at this point, the branch
snaps right off); a neat final cut
at the collar to finish.

❑ *Check when completed*

❧ TIP 51 ❧

If you haven't already done so, go ahead and direct-sow seeds of favorite vegetables, including peas and kale, directly into prepared garden soil. Cover them over after planting, and be diligent about watering regularly so they can germinate.

☐ *Check when completed*

❧ TIP 52 ❧

Trim your evergreen hedge
before it really starts growing for the
year. Remove old stems at their
bases. Shorten others that are too
long. Shape so that the top of the
plant—when viewed from the
side—is narrower than the base.
This not only looks better but
is easier to maintain.

☐ *Check when completed*

❧ TIP 53 ❧

Plant herbs, in the ground, in pots, or in windowboxes. Wherever you grow them, make sure they have decent soil. It does not have to be especially dark and rich (which can lead to overly lush or lanky growth), but it should be well drained to prevent root rot. Adding pumice to soil helps drainage.

☐ *Check when completed*

❦ TIP 54 ❦

As its buds begin to open,
protect your flowering dogwood
against the dreaded anthracnose
disease. Contact your nearest
Cooperative Extension service, or
ask an arborist to find out what they
consider the most effective
fungicide. You may have to treat
the tree more than once.

❑ *Check when completed*

❧ TIP 55 ❧

Now is the time to plant
your summer bulbs—such as
dahlias, galtonias, crocosmia, and
glads. These like organically rich,
well-drained soil and a spot
with plenty of sunshine. Also,
assuming you are growing the tall
kinds, place them where they won't
block other plants from view.

☐ *Check when completed*

❧ TIP 56 ❧

While rains should irrigate the
lawn for you this time of year, they
also make it grow like gangbusters.
Mow regularly so the job doesn't
get away from you. Also, when you
mow more often, you can leave
the shorter clippings right on the
lawn to break down. They add
nitrogen to the soil.

☐ *Check when completed*

❧ TIP 57 ❧

Allow wildflowers to go to
seed and try collecting the seed
yourself for later replanting. Pick
the stalks and hang them upside
down in a warm, dark place. If the
flower heads are the sort that
"shatters," simply bag the tops in
order to capture falling seeds.

☐ *Check when completed*

✦ TIP 58 ✦

Leave fading bulb foliage alone
so it can send nutrients down into
the bulb below to fuel next year's
show. The leaves will yellow
and flag, and no, the process isn't
pretty. Bending over handfuls
and cinching them with a rubber
band has no benefits (and in fact,
may be detrimental to the bulbs),
though it looks slightly better.

☐ *Check when completed*

❧ TIP 59 ❧

Get in the habit of forming a basin for every plant you install or move. It should be around the perimeter of the plant's topgrowth "drip line" (the outer edge). Mound soil up a few inches in a circle around the plant. Then, when you water, it will go straight to the roots. A basin also holds mulch well.

☐ *Check when completed*

❧ TIP 60 ❧

Make a mini water garden in a
tub or kettle. It must be 18 inches
deep to host a potted water lily
(ask the nursery about ones that do
well in smaller quarters). Or try
other attractive aquatics, both
floaters and tall ones like irises and
papyrus. Full sun is best. Top off the
water when it evaporates a bit.

☐ *Check when completed*

❦ TIP 61 ❦

Vegetable garden growing too
slowly? Leaves looking a bit yellow?
Apply a sidedressing of higher
nitrogen fertilizer to give the plants
a boost (be careful not to get any
directly on the plants). Crops that
respond really well to this treatment
include broccoli, cabbage,
cauliflower, chard, and lettuce.

☐ *Check when completed*

❧ TIP 62 ❧

Deadhead both annuals and
perennials. That is, pinch or cut off
spent flowers promptly. Otherwise,
the plants may be tempted to
spend a lot of energy going to seed
and the flower show will end. This
way, you persuade them to redirect
their energy into making a fresh
round of flowers.

❑ *Check when completed*

❧ TIP 63 ❧

Lay the groundwork for a
bountiful herb harvest later in the
year. In a bright, sunny spot—
ideally, not far from your kitchen—
create a raised bed or prepare
various pots with well-drained,
organically rich soil. Fill with
seedlings of parsley, sage, oregano,
thyme, chives, and cilantro.

❑ *Check when completed*

❖ TIP 64 ❖

Rains are tapering off, so you have to do more watering. For shrubs and trees, a slow, deep soaking is much better than occasional lighter sprinklings. Set the hose or soaker hose at the plant's base, at a slow trickle, for an hour. Check with a trowel to see whether moisture has penetrated. If not, water for another hour or until satisfied.

☐ *Check when completed*

❧ TIP 65 ❧

If you weren't happy with the location or numbers of some of your spring bulbs, it is safe to dig them up and move them elsewhere in the yard. Their foliage should have died down by now, or nearly so, and thus they should be practically dormant—an optimum time to make your move.

☐ *Check when completed*

✤ TIP 66 ✤

Slugs are rampant. They
especially love shade perennials,
as much for the succulence
of the leaves as for the moist,
sheltered environment. You might
consider reducing or taking away
mulch—at least for now—to
reduce hiding places for them.

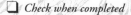 *Check when completed*

❦ TIP 67 ❦

Plant warm-season vegetables
now in an area that is well prepared
with moisture-retaining organic
matter. Raised beds are ideal.
Vegetables that prosper in warm
garden soil include corn, sweet and
hot peppers, squash, and tomatoes.

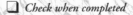 *Check when completed*

❧ TIP 68 ❧

Plant heat-loving annuals.
There should be plenty for sale at
local outlets—portulaca, verbena,
and salvia are favorites. Larger
plants, while a bit more expensive,
have a better chance of doing well
this time of year. In any event,
water them upon planting and
often as rains diminish.

❑ *Check when completed*

❧ TIP 69 ❧

As spring winds down, assess your various spring-flowering shrubs. Did you like the flowers? Do they complement the rest of your garden in terms of color and form? Are you bored of rhododendrons and camellias? Take this opportunity to research replacement plants you might want and make plans to "shake things up" later.

☐ *Check when completed*

❧ Tip 70 ❧

You may spy the white froth of spittlebugs on many of your flowers around this time. The actual bugs are hidden underneath; they're tiny green nymphs. Actually, they are not harmful . . . but if the appearance bothers you or many plants are affected, rinse the spittle off with a jet from the hose.

☐ *Check when completed*

❧ TIP 71 ❧

Visit the shrubs, rosebushes,
and trees that you planted this
spring and give each one a tune-up.
(You should already be supplying
good soaking waterings.) Check for
signs of disease and insect pests. Cut
off any afflicted plant parts and get
rid of them. (But save a small
amount if you need a diagnosis and
advice on treatment.)

☐ *Check when completed*

❧ TIP 72 ❧

Always make pruning cuts on an angle. That way, water will be more likely to run off, rather than collecting on the cut area and causing rot or disease. A slanted cut also dries out faster after a rain. Last but not least, this leaves a smaller stub, which is better for the plant's appearance.

☐ *Check when completed*

❧ TIP 73 ❧

Set out a rain barrel. This is a
thrifty way to collect free water for
your garden. You won't be able
to move it later—too heavy—so
choose a spot where branches or
buildings won't obstruct it, and
where it won't be in the way. Place
a screen over the top to keep out
debris, bugs, and dirt.

❏ *Check when completed*

❖ TIP 74 ❖

In your shade garden, as the ground gets drier, bleeding heart, corydalis, and other perennials tend to throw in the towel. With their flowering done, the stems and leaves start to yellow. There is no reason to watch and wait. Take sharp clippers and cut everything down to the ground. Don't worry; the plants will return in glory next spring.

☐ *Check when completed*

❧ TIP 75 ❧

Blackspot may be marring your
rosebush leaves. Promptly pick off
all affected foliage and get rid of it
(do not add it to the compost pile).
Prune the bush to improve air
circulation. And deliver water to the
soil; never let it splash on the leaves.
In severe cases, spray.

☐ *Check when completed*

❧ TIP 76 ❧

After setting out tomatoes, provide support. If the plant is not too bushy yet, installing a tomato cage will help improve air circulation. Also be sure to water right at ground level; never let water splash up onto the leaves, which can lead to disease.

☐ *Check when completed*

❧ TIP 77 ❧

Have your marigolds turned
to lace? If so, suspect slugs. Go on a
night safari to see what's eating
them. If it is slugs, try the beer trick.
Place a shallow dish filled with stale
beer by the plants; by morning, any
slugs attracted to the beer will be
drowned or too drunk to care.

☐ *Check when completed*

✤ TIP 78 ✤

Keep cats from treating your flowerbeds like a litter box! Lay down some chicken wire and cover it lightly with soil or mulch—they don't like the way their paws get snagged. Alternatively, try sprinkling an unpleasant-smelling repellent around: hot pepper, black pepper, citronella oil, even coffee grounds.

❑ *Check when completed*

❧ TIP 79 ❧

Wilder areas of the yard may need some attention. Congested, overcrowded conditions are not good for the health of the plants as they compete for resources. Wildflowers may get lanky and not bloom as well. Just do some judicious thinning and toss the discards on the compost pile.

☐ *Check when completed*

❧ TIP 80 ❧

Like your evergreens neat?
Trim now, shearing back new
growth (the candles, in the case of
pines) before it is fully expanded.
Don't make severe cuts, just shaping
ones, at this time. This also helps
keep the plants in bounds and
inspires them to grow more densely.

☐ *Check when completed*

❖ TIP 81 ❖

Keep after those weeds! Knock
down carpets of smaller ones with a
hoe—make sure it's sharp, and it
will do an impressive job.
Otherwise, hand-pull individual
ones. Mulch after weeding to help
keep weed growth down.

☐ *Check when completed*

❖ TIP 82 ❖

If you are growing leafy
herbs for harvest, prevent them
from going to seed by pinching off
flowers when they develop. This
forces the plants to continue
producing tasty leaves and prevents
self-sowing. Last but not least, it
thwarts bees, which are more
interested in the flowers than any
other part of the plant, of course.

☐ *Check when completed*

❧ TIP 83 ❧

Look before you squish a
garden bug! Not all are harmful
pests. When in doubt as to
a critter's identity, look him up in
gardening books or take one
(in a jar) to a garden center staffer or
Cooperative Extension office. If
it is a pest, you can get advice on
how to combat it.

☐ *Check when completed*

❧ TIP 84 ❧

Berry plants will soon start to
ripen their sweet harvest. But there's
competition for the fruit—birds,
wild animals perhaps, and various
insect pests. Luckily, they can all be
thwarted the same way, if you act
early. Drape the plants in netting;
garden-supply shops and mail-order
suppliers sell large-enough pieces
with the right mesh.

☐ *Check when completed*

❧ TIP 85 ❧

When you pick peonies for
bouquets, check for ants before you
bring them into the house. They
aren't nibbling on the plant, but
rather going after the sticky, sweet
stuff that drips from the buds. But
they also lodge inside the leaves and
open blossoms. Just shake each
blossom vigorously to evict them, or
swish in a bucket of water.

❑ *Check when completed*

❧ TIP 86 ❧

Mulch around the bases of your perennials, or renew depleted mulch. A good mulch layer helps keep burgeoning weed populations at bay and helps retain soil moisture. Be careful, however, not to push the mulch flush up against the stems or crown of the plant, which can invite rot.

☐ *Check when completed*

❧ TIP 87 ❧

Here's a clever way to water
hanging baskets or other potted
plants, especially when you
won't be around to attend to them
on a hot day. Set a few ice
cubes on their surface before you
leave the house. These will melt
gradually over the course of the day,
gradually soaking in.

☐ *Check when completed*

❧ TIP 88 ❧

Float rose petals in a punch or
sangria, or scatter them over
buttercream-frosted cake or cupcakes.
Pick them on a hot afternoon when
the fragrance is at its peak; rinse
them gently (especially important if
you have sprayed your rosebushes
with anything), pat dry, then store in
a plastic bag in the refrigerator for a
few hours before using.

☐ *Check when completed*

✤ TIP 89 ✤

Keep pots of herbs near the kitchen
for spontaneous summer meals.
Ones that do well in a container
include rosemary, cilantro, sage,
parsley, oregano, chives, and thyme.
Water in the morning and cut that
same evening for maximum flavor;
cut only as much as you need. Rinse
off any dust or dirt before using.

☐ *Check when completed*

❧ TIP 90 ❧

Now is the time to take a close
look at the fruit trees you pruned
earlier. Sometimes those cuts
stimulate unwanted shoots. Catch
them while they're young, and it's
no big deal to simply rub them off
with a gloved hand—and the
problem is solved!

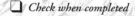 *Check when completed*

❧ SUMMER ❧

❧ EVERYDAY TIP ❧

Enjoy your garden. In the
midst of chores and to-do lists, you
might overlook why it's such a
pleasure. Sit outside, read a book,
take a stroll, snooze in a hammock,
have a party—reap the rewards.

❧ TIP 91 ❧

Plant some annuals now that
both air and soil are warm enough.
But avoid the temptation
to buy blooming plants—the
transition from their pampered life
at the garden center to your
yard may cause them to drop their
petals. They'll recover, of course.
But it's smarter to buy annuals with
plenty of good buds.

☐ *Check when completed*

❧ TIP 92 ❧

Move potted houseplants outside
to a patio or deck for summer. The
fresh air and bright sunshine will do
them good. But make the transition
gradual. If they get too much sun at
first, you'll observe brown patches
on the leaves which is, yes, sunburn.
Better to set them in part-day sun at
first and see how they do.

☐ *Check when completed*

❧ TIP 93 ❧

If a weed problem has gotten
out of hand and you are ready to
resort to herbicides (weed killer), do
so with care. Choose the least-toxic
chemical possible. Then spray on a
dry, windless day. As a precaution,
protect nearby desirable plants
temporarily with plastic or a tarp.

 *Check when completed*

❧ TIP 94 ❧

Get more shrubs from midsummer's "semi-hardwood" cuttings. These root easily and grow into young plants by fall. Dust the base of pencil-thin shoots with rooting powder, then plant in light, organically rich ground. Water gently and often—they should root in four to six weeks. Good candidates: mock orange, buddleia, viburnum, kerria.

☐ *Check when completed*

❧ TIP 95 ❧

Deadhead your annuals.
That is, pinch or cut off spent
flowers promptly. Otherwise, the
plants may be tempted to spend a
lot of energy going to seed and the
flower show will end. This way, you
might persuade them to redirect
their energy into making a fresh
round of flowers.

☐ *Check when completed*

❧ TIP 96 ❧

Check on your compost pile.
Hot weather causes the contents to
break down faster, and you may
find you have a bounty of "black
gold." If you don't use it, it will
continue to break down. Instead,
scoop it out from the bottom
and use it around the yard as a
nourishing mulch.

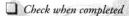 *Check when completed*

❧ TIP 97 ❧

It's a good idea to feed your rosebushes this month. Granular types that are made especially for roses are your best bet. Just sprinkle them on the ground; consult the label to figure out how much. Make sure to soak the plants before and after, if rainfall is sparse.

 *Check when completed*

❖ TIP 98 ❖

Make a ring or basin around
the bases of your ornamental trees.
This has several benefits. It holds
water well so moisture can be
delivered straight down to the root
system; it also holds mulch in place.
And its presence will remind you to
keep the lawnmower and weed-
whacker a safe distance away.

☐ *Check when completed*

❧ TIP 99 ❧

Do poppies make poor bouquet flowers? Not true! It's just that sap dripping from the bottom fouls vase water. Use the florist trick. Pick them in their full glory (or slightly before) and seal the cut ends: Dip them in boiling water for 30 seconds, or singe the ends with a candle or match.

☐ *Check when completed*

❧ TIP 100 ❧

Walk through and double-check all
your plant supports, from tomato
cages to staked hollyhocks. Rampant
growth and full weight may have
caused them to lean or pulled them
down. Reinsert stakes securely into
the ground, replace missing ties, and
add more ties as needed. In other
words, reestablish order.

☐ *Check when completed*

❧ TIP 101 ❧

The weed wars are far from over. Under no circumstances should you let annual weeds go to seed! This is how they create a population explosion. Perennial weeds will keep on spreading if you don't stop them. Thwart all of them by chopping off their heads, yanking them out, or both.

❑ *Check when completed*

❧ TIP 102 ❧

Install a new brick or flagstone
path—a much easier job in dry
weather. Carve out the course with a
shovel to a depth of several inches,
then fill with a base of sand or sand
dust. Wiggle the bricks or stones
into place, separating them by an
inch or less. Water down, let settle,
add more sand if needed.

☐ *Check when completed*

⚜ TIP 103 ⚜

Algae problem in your birdbath?
Assuming you've cleaned it (a
mixture of equal parts of vinegar
and water works well and is
nontoxic for the birds), there's one
other thing you can try. Pick about
six stems off your lavender plant,
wrap them with a rubber band, and
float the bundle in the water.

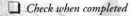 *Check when completed*

❧ TIP 104 ❧

Sketch or photograph your
flowerbeds when they are at their
peak. Not only will the images be a
source of pride, but they'll also
provide useful information when
you view them with care later. You'll
be able to identify successful
combinations, as well as ones that
didn't work out—all fodder for
deciding on next year's plans.

☐ *Check when completed*

✤ TIP 105 ✤

In warm summer weather, hanging
baskets (and other containers) dry
out amazingly quickly. Use a
watering wand to soak hanging
baskets thoroughly in the mornings.
If you haven't already done so, add a
"mulch" of dampened moss, an inch
or so thick. Just scoot it aside when
watering and replace it after.

☐ *Check when completed*

❧ TIP 106 ❧

Pick bouquets often! It's one of the great rewards of gardening; plus the very process of going out and selecting flowers compels you to examine—and enjoy—your plants as you go by. Bring a water bucket and plunk in the stems as you go. This keeps everything fresh until you get inside, where you can groom and shorten each stem.

☐ *Check when completed*

✤ TIP 107 ✤

Keep your shrub and hedge
areas weeded so that the plants you
want can avail themselves of the
water and soil nutrients. If the
ground is a bit too dry for easy
weed-pulling, shave annual weeds
off at soil level and smother them
with a few inches of mulch.

☐ *Check when completed*

✤ TIP 108 ✤

Pinch back young mum plants now. Though it seems brutal, this operation causes them to grow shorter but bushier (left alone, they can get leggy and fall over). They will bloom a bit later as a result, but the plants will be stronger.

☐ *Check when completed*

❧ TIP 109 ❧

Mow the lawn less often during dry
weather spells. When you do mow,
set the mower blades higher to help
keep the grasses green and allow
grass blades to shade out low-
growing weeds. (Taller types tend to
develop deeper roots.) Don't bother
with raking—if you mow often
enough, the clippings will be small
enough to break down on site.

☐ *Check when completed*

❧ TIP 110 ❧

Cherry trees ought to be bearing
about this time. Wait till the
color is good before picking. If you
miss the boat and ripe fruit falls
on the ground, snag it right away. It
may be just fine. If you leave it
there, it's only going to rot.

☐ *Check when completed*

✤ TIP III ✤

A whitefly problem can develop if
you have potted plants in a
warm corner of the porch or deck.
One wave of your hand will
send up a cloud of these foliage-
sucking beasties. Fight back with
sprays from the hose. Segregate
affected plants, so you can treat
them individually and also to
improve air circulation.

☐ *Check when completed*

❧ TIP 112 ❧

If you haven't done so already, go
out and clip off all spent, browned
flowers on your shrubs. They
really detract from the appearance,
and they drain energy from the
plant as they attempt to go to seed.
If you don't do this, they'll hang
around all summer and all winter
and detract from next spring's show.

☐ *Check when completed*

❦ TIP 113 ❦

Some plants develop powdery
mildew in midsummer, thanks to
the heat and humidity. In particular,
the leaves of lilacs, roses, phlox,
and bee balm turn powdery white.
There's not much you can do,
except try to improve air circulation
within and around the plants with a
little judicious clipping. In the
future, seek out resistant varieties.

☐ *Check when completed*

❧ TIP 114 ❧

Beat the heat for your potted plants.
Hard surfaces such as the patio,
deck, or steps absorb a lot of solar
energy (especially dark or
brick surfaces), which is radiated
back with a vengeance and can
literally bake your plants. Watering
helps, but you may also have to
temporarily move pots to the edges
or to somewhat shadier settings.

☐ *Check when completed*

⚜ TIP 115 ⚜

Plan a Fourth of July patriotic
flower display. Get some red or blue
pots. Then fill the red ones with
blue and white annuals, and the
blue ones with red and white
flowers. Group them together—on
the front steps to welcome visitors
or to the side on the patio or deck
where they can be admired.

❑ *Check when completed*

❖ TIP 116 ❖

Harvest your cucumbers, squash, and zucchini on an almost daily basis. This practice encourages more production; plus you don't want them to rot on the vine. Donate your surplus to a local food bank (they usually get canned goods— homegrown produce will be a treat).

☐ *Check when completed*

❧ TIP 117 ❧

Mail-order bulb catalogs are on hand now, or you can shop via the Internet. These outlets will afford you a far broader selection of interesting and colorful spring-flowering bulbs than you'd ever see at a garden center, so feast your imagination on the enticing offerings. Order now so you'll get them in time for fall planting.

☐ *Check when completed*

❧ TIP 118 ❧

As soon as perennial flowers or
stems start to die back, cut them
back to live growth. This not
only improves their appearance, but
helps prevent insect pests and
diseases from moving in. And it will
encourage some plants to rebloom
later in the season. Cut-and-come-
again favorites include yarrow,
daisies, and delphiniums.

☐ *Check when completed*

❖ TIP 119 ❖

Favorite annuals (California poppy, cosmos) going to seed? If you like them, let them, and you'll have a crowd next year. But a couple should be reined in, before it's too late, by clipping off their fading flowers or developing seedheads: four o'clocks (self-sown ones never seem to have the same pretty colors) and foxgloves (poisonous to animals).

☐ *Check when completed*

❧ TIP 120 ❧

Dried flowers for arrangements
and craft projects are easy to make.
Just remember that whatever form
or stage the blooms are in,
that's how they'll dry, with no
changes. Array them on screens
in a hot, dry, well-ventilated room.
Or place them in plastic boxes of
silica gel for a few days.

☐ *Check when completed*

❧ TIP 121 ❧

Do not fertilize your rosebushes
after mid-July, or they'll have
reduced winter hardiness. Also, late
doses inspire a burst of soft
green growth that will be vulnerable
to frost. Enjoy the remaining
buds and blossoms—in the garden
or in bouquets. Deadhead to
encourage rebloom on hybrid teas
and English roses.

☐ *Check when completed*

❧ TIP 122 ❧

Growing some tender, tropical
plants, in the ground or in pots?
They will thrive in the height
of summer, but only if you don't
neglect watering. You also ought to
give them a good dose of fertilizer
once a month, just to pump up the
show (always apply according
to label directions).

☐ *Check when completed*

❧ TIP 123 ❧

Any signs of distress in your shrubs right now may be attributed to drought stress. Of course, occasional deep soakings will bring some relief. You might also hose down the entire plant, in an effort both to cool it off and to dislodge pests like spider mites.

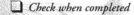 *Check when completed*

❧ TIP 124 ❧

Even succulents and native
plants can struggle if rains cease and
hot weather lingers. Newly planted
ones will appreciate a little shade—
move potted ones to a shadier spot.
Water every three weeks to a
month, as needed.

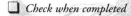

☐ *Check when completed*

❧ TIP 125 ❧

Don't forget that established trees may appreciate some supplemental water by midsummer, particularly if the weather remains hot and dry. Set a hose at the base and let the water soak in slowly—this could literally take hours. Check back occasionally to make sure the water isn't just running off the soil surface.

☐ *Check when completed*

❧ TIP 126 ❧

You may feed your rosebushes
now, for what is likely the last time
of this calendar year. If it hasn't
rained, be sure to soak the soil
before and after applying the
fertilizer. Use a product labeled
especially for roses, and follow the
directions carefully—more
is not better.

☐ *Check when completed*

JULY

❖ TIP 127 ❖

Visit the garden center for
midsummer bargains. The crowds
are gone, and the offerings may be
depleted, but sometimes you can
score good deals on larger plants.
Just remember that anything you
plant now will need extra water and
attention to survive the stress of
being moved in the heat.

☐ *Check when completed*

❧ TIP 128 ❧

Water the lawn in the morning.
This gives the grass roots time to
absorb the moisture before the day's
heat steals some due to evaporation.
It's also better than afternoon or
evening watering because, at those
times, moisture can linger and
encourage the development
of fungal diseases.

☐ *Check when completed*

JULY

❧ TIP 129 ❧

Pay a visit to your established
vines. If flowering is substantially
over, you can cut to shape the
plant; be sure your clippers are sharp
so you don't mash the stems. Either
chop off wayward stems or fasten
them to the support with soft ties.

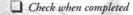 ☐ *Check when completed*

❖ TIP 130 ❖

Certain vegetables can be
sown directly into the vegetable
garden right about now, and they
will produce a good harvest well
before the really cold weather
arrives. The best choices are edible-
root crops such as carrots, radishes,
and turnips. Remember, regular
watering is the key.

❑ *Check when completed*

❧ TIP 131 ❧

Now is the time to plant another installation of glad corms—no later, if you want blooms in late August and early September. Stagger the plantings so you will have blooms at various times—it's more fun that way. Set them about 4 inches deep, and don't forget the stakes.

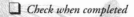 ☐ *Check when completed*

❧ TIP 132 ❧

Container roses, including those cute little miniature ones, may still be for sale. Don't plant them in the ground right now. Just keep them in a spot that receives about 6 hours of sun a day, and keep up the water so they don't suffer in the heat (pile mulch around them for protection). You can put them in the ground later, when cool weather returns.

☐ *Check when completed*

❖ TIP 133 ❖

Pick a water lily bouquet!
As you may have noticed, the
blooms last around three days
in a garden pool. And they do the
same in a vase indoors. They
even close up each evening and
reopen each morning. Be sure to
change the water daily.

☐ *Check when completed*

❧ TIP 134 ❧

Lift up and look under your potted plants. If the contents have been thriving, roots may have filled the entire container and be clogging the drainage holes. If water cannot drain properly, performance declines and root rot can follow. Two solutions: repot the contents in something larger, or remove a plant or two.

☐ *Check when completed*

❧ TIP 135 ❧

Summer-blooming wildflowers
are going to seed. Clip them off and
dry them, collecting the seeds for
future use. Store them in a cool, dry,
dark place so they don't germinate
too soon. Plan to sow them
later in the fall or early next year—
write yourself a reminder.

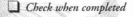 *Check when completed*

❧ TIP 136 ❧

Pick and dry fragrant herbs—it's one of gardening's most enchanting chores. Pick lush stems whose blossoms have formed but not yet opened, for maximum scent and flavor. Rinse them quickly and thoroughly pat dry. Make bundles and hang them upside-down in a hot, dark spot, such as an attic. This way, they'll dry before they can rot.

☐ *Check when completed*

❧ TIP 137 ❧

Is the surface of your soil repelling water when you irrigate? You can try two things to remedy this distressing situation. Water slower or more lightly in the hopes that it will sink in better. Or add a surfactant, such as saponin (available at garden centers) to the water; it goes in a siphoning device connected to your hose.

☐ *Check when completed*

❧ TIP 138 ❧

Deadhead perennials that are
still generating blooms. This
inspires the plants to keep going.
Also, trimming or pinching back
the ends of stems encourages the
plant to grow a bit more compactly.
You can take out spent inner
stems, though, as these are no
longer productive.

☐ *Check when completed*

❧ TIP 139 ❧

Deter tunneling rodents. Start
with the milder war tactics, such as
flooding the tunnels and setting
out smelly repellents. If that fails, go
get some traps. Note that traps
that capture them alive (for release
far from your house!) may or may
not be allowed; check with your
local Fish and Game Department.

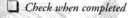 ❑ *Check when completed*

❧ TIP 140 ❧

Scout your plants for aphids.
Outbreaks occur in dry, as well as
moist, conditions, and you must
intervene before everything gets
covered and infested. Luckily, if you
notice them early, all you really
have to do is evict them with a stiff
spray from the hose or use a mild
soap-based insecticide.

☐ *Check when completed*

⚜ TIP 141 ⚜

Weed-whacking is not a fun chore, but these tips will make the project faster and more efficient. If possible, work in the late afternoon, past the heat of the day, when the plants are drier. Make sure the tool is clean and you have fresh "string" reeled out several inches. Wear socks, long pants, and eye protection.

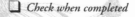 *Check when completed*

❧ TIP 142 ❧

Before you go on vacation,
check your watering systems very
carefully—even if you have timers
and everything is self-regulating.
(If you have a sophisticated
in-ground system, it would be
worthwhile to call the contractor
who installed it and ask them to
come over for a "tune-up.")

☐ *Check when completed*

❧ TIP 143 ❧

This time of year, be sure always to apply water to the ground right at the base of plants. Doing this not only delivers it to the roots more efficiently than overhead watering, but prevents diseases that can occur when hot weather and damp foliage collide.

☐ *Check when completed*

❧ TIP 144 ❧

Pick some roses! Cut just as
buds are showing color so they can
unfurl their beauty—and
fragrance—indoors. Take long
stems, which you can always shorten
when you recut for the vase. If
feasible, recut the stems underwater
in the sink or a bowl; this florist's
trick ensures that the stem is full of
water, with no air bubbles.

☐ *Check when completed*

❧ TIP 145 ❧

Some of the taller-growing annuals, such as sunflowers, cleome, and cosmos, benefit from staking. Better late than never! Just march out into the yard with a few bamboo stakes and some ties and take care of it. Otherwise a windy day or a summer storm is sure to flatten them.

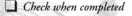 *Check when completed*

❖ TIP 146 ❖

Growing dahlias? To assure
a great show later in the summer
and on into the fall, you need to
take good care of the plants right
now. This means regular water as
well as some fertilizer. Watch out for
aphids, which relish the new
growth—if you spot them, blast
them off with the hose.

☐ *Check when completed*

❖ Tip 147 ❖

When weather starts to get hotter,
watering often, and enough, can
become a real chore. Get some
soaker hoses and thread them
through the flowerbeds, groundcover area, vegetable garden, or any
other spot that needs regular
moisture. For these, as well as for
sprinklers, consider investing in a
timer that installs at the faucet.

☐ *Check when completed*

❖ TIP 148 ❖

Deadhead snapdragons once the flower stalks have finished blooming. Often, this inspires the plants to produce a second round of blooms—especially if you remember to keep on watering the plants so they have the energy they need to make that encore performance.

☐ *Check when completed*

❧ TIP 149 ❧

Protect ripening fruit
such as strawberries and blueberries
from marauding birds. Some
or all of the following protective
tactics are worth a try: netting
made for this purpose, mylar
balloons, and strips of glittering
aluminum foil.

☐ *Check when completed*

❧ TIP 150 ❧

Wait to harvest your
blueberries until they are fully
blue—for at least a week. A little
more time on the bush and in the
sun makes for a richer, deeper,
sweeter flavor. Then pick them early
in the day, after any dew has dried.
The white cast on blueberry skin is
normal and natural.

☐ *Check when completed*

❖ TIP 151 ❖

Thirsty groundcovers may
need your attention. To maximize
water uptake, irrigate early on a
windless day, and wet the area to a
depth of several inches. Note that
the ones growing in full sun show
their distress sooner, but ones in
shade suffer also.

☐ *Check when completed*

❧ TIP 152 ❧

Garlic is ready for you to
harvest it when the tops begin to
yellow, flag, and die down. But
just to make sure, dig under and
take out a sample. You want to
see plump bulbs encased in a good,
papery covering. Brush off the
dirt, and store the bulbs in a
cool, dry location.

☐ *Check when completed*

❧ TIP 153 ❧

Visit the vegetable garden and tidy up. Pull out spent plants. Scoop up plant debris from the bases of plants that are still growing, and pinch off dead or yellowing foliage. Remove and discard damaged and overripe fruits, from the plants as well as the ground—this stuff only encourages insect pests.

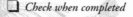 ☐ *Check when completed*

❧ TIP 154 ❧

Remove suckers from your apple
and crabapple trees—suckers both
divert energy from the tree and
detract from its appearance. Gently
digging down to the source of the
sucker, with your fingers or a trowel,
will provide more complete removal
than just lopping it off.

☐ *Check when completed*

❧ TIP 155 ❧

Make yourself leave alone those
perennials that are winding down. If
you cut them back too soon or
remove foliage that has not fully
yellowed and fallen over, you are
depriving the root systems of
nutrients that are being passed
down now. Be patient—your reward
will come next year!

☐ *Check when completed*

❧ TIP 156 ❧

Extra water is critical when
there is little or no rain. Water
deeply and regularly at the bases of
the plants, where possible. While
it can be wasteful, overhead
sprinkler watering does help reduce
heat stress by lowering leaf
temperatures. In any event, irrigate
in the morning or evening to avoid
losing moisture to evaporation.

☐ *Check when completed*

❀ TIP 157 ❀

Don't pinch your mums any more now. Let them grow freely so that they will be of substantial size and develop good buds for a colorful fall display. As this process goes forward, remember to keep the plants evenly moist for a better quality flower show.

☐ *Check when completed*

❧ TIP 158 ❧

Rebuild or even expand the
watering basins around the bases
of your trees and shrubs, in
anticipation of winter rains. Ideally,
a basin should be as far out as the
"drip line" (farthest extent of the
plant's canopy)—or even a bit
farther. Put compost or another
mulch in the basin.

❑ *Check when completed*

❧ TIP 159 ❧

Tidy climbing roses as their
blooming slows. Take out old wood,
which is gray rather than brown
or green. Dead, damaged, and
diseased wood should also be taken
out. Retie canes to supports for
storm protection.

☐ *Check when completed*

❧ TIP 160 ❧

Going on vacation? Find someone to care for your yard and plants while you are away—ideally, another gardener who understands what needs to be done (watering, mainly). If you want to try a clever slow-watering gadget, better try it out ahead of time to make sure it works.

☐ *Check when completed*

❧ TIP 161 ❧

Visit the local garden center
to see what's on sale. Protect any
newly purchased plants from
drying out by mulching. You can
often load up on various pots and
containers, and maybe even some
garden ornaments.

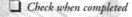 *Check when completed*

❦ TIP 162 ❦

Now is the time to renew
the organic matter in the tidied-up
vegetable garden and in the now-
emptied flowerbeds. Well-rotted
compost is ideal, or you can
buy bagged compost or use
dehydrated cow manure. Dig and
mix everything to a depth of
6 or more inches.

☐ *Check when completed*

❧ TIP 163 ❧

The best time to harvest herbs is right before their flowers open. Their essential oils will be at their peak. Examples include mint, thyme, basil, angelica, and epazote. Cut in late morning, after the dew has dried but before the hot midday sun bakes the flavor out of the leaves.

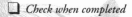 *Check when completed*

❧ TIP 164 ❧

Help out your potted plants.
Those in clay pots, especially, have
trouble holding onto necessary
moisture. Water in the morning
hours and again in the evening.
Sprinkle the plants lightly during
the day, which mainly just slows
evaporation and cools off the plants
a bit. And if possible, move them
out of strong light.

☐ *Check when completed*

❧ TIP 165 ❧

Time to give rampant-growing
shrubs and hedges another haircut!
Use freshly sharpened clippers and
loppers. If the plants are thorny or
twiggy, wear a long-sleeved shirt and
tough gloves as you work. Remove
suckers emerging from the bases.
Clip back new growth all around to
inspire a thicker profile.

☐ *Check when completed*

❧ TIP 166 ❧

Hot weather causes the compost pile to go into overdrive, provided you keep it moist. So stop by with the hose every now and then and give it a soaking. Then stir, using a long stick or a tool handle. Adding coffee grounds and tea leaves seems to help accelerate the decomposition activity.

☐ *Check when completed*

❧ TIP 167 ❧

Flowering annuals may be the main, or at least, freshest source of garden color right now. So take good care of them. Pinch off spent flowers, and yellowing or spent leaves. Water regularly so they can continue to be productive. Potted ones are especially vulnerable to drying out.

☐ *Check when completed*

❧ TIP 168 ❧

Plan ahead for welcome fall
color by planting some fall crocus
now. It's not actually a true
crocus, though it looks a bit similar
in size and form; it only comes
in pink and white. (The Latin name
is *Colchicum*.) Plant the bulbs
about three inches down, in good
soil, in full sun.

☐ *Check when completed*

❧ TIP 169 ❧

You can continue to either
pick rose bouquets or deadhead the
plants. Despite the weather and all
the insects and diseases that some
roses attract, they are wonderfully
willing to keep on pumping out the
flowers. Keeping the plants watered
and mulched will also help.

 *Check when completed*

❧ TIP 170 ❧

Examine the base of your fruit trees. If suckers are originating from the rootstock, the trees will never produce viable fruit. Pull them out if possible, by cutting them away, using a sharp pair of clippers or loppers. A callus will develop, so it is not necessary to paint over the wound.

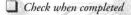 *Check when completed*

❧ TIP 171 ❧

Check on your rain barrel.
Empty any lingering water
somewhere it can be used. Then
scrub out the interior with a stiff
brush to remove any algae or other
crud. Return it to its spot and be
sure to cover it with a screen to keep
out debris and bugs. Fall rains
should soon refill it.

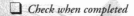 *Check when completed*

❧ TIP 172 ❧

Annuals that have been blooming
all summer may now be running out
of steam. Others, such as geraniums
and petunias, can be revived and
persuaded to make an encore
performance if you clip them back
and keep on watering. All the
rest, sadly, ought to come out and
be sent to the compost pile.

❏ *Check when completed*

❧ TIP 173 ❧

Coleus plants, in the ground
or in pots, are real troopers. Reward
their hard work by continuing to
give them good care. Pinch off their
tops from time to time to encourage
bushy growth. Clear away fallen
leaves from the bases of the plants.
Water regularly and deeply.

☐ *Check when completed*

✤ TIP 174 ✤

Give dusty shrubs in the yard a
brief but beneficial bath. Walk
around with the hose, with a fan-
sprinkler attachment, and douse
both sides of the leaves. The tops
may look like they need it the most,
but don't forget to spray the
bottoms, as well. This allows better
intake of moisture and air.

☐ *Check when completed*

❧ TIP 175 ❧

Shrub roses and old-fashioned
varieties often develop bright and
attractive fruits called "rose hips." If
you like the look (or if you want to
harvest them to make a tea rich in
Vitamin C), stop deadheading these
bushes—that will give the hips a
chance to develop.

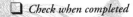 *Check when completed*

❧ TIP 176 ❧

Spend a little time on your rosebushes today, with the twin aims of not only improving their looks, but also preventing insect and disease problems. Get rid of yellowed or diseased leaves, and be sure to clean up any that have fallen on the ground under the plants.

☐ *Check when completed*

❧ TIP 177 ❧

Dormant sections of the yard
can be improved now. Work during
the cooler parts of the day, and dig
and hack out all growth and
obstructions, including all roots and
rocks. Depending on what you
hope to grow, till down to a depth
of 6 to 12 inches, and add plenty
of organic matter.

☐ *Check when completed*

❧ TIP 178 ❧

Some fall bloomers will not form buds—and thus turn in a disappointing performance, if you do not water them now. Asters, mums, and dahlias are classic examples. Irrigate them often—and consistently. Verify that the water is actually reaching the root zone by digging down to check.

☐ *Check when completed*

❧ TIP 179 ❧

Orchids that have finished
blooming will want a rest. Floral
stalks that turn brown all the
way back to the main stem are spent
and can be clipped off. If the
plant put on a lot of growth and
now looks dense or crowded,
you can repot.

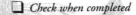 *Check when completed*

❧ TIP 180 ❧

It's time to pick your glads!
Make your move when the first few
buds at the bottom of the spike
are completely open but the rest are
still in bud. (Leave foliage on
the plant; it replenishes the corm for
next year's show.) Recut the
stems indoors, and put them in a
vase of lukewarm water; change
the water daily.

❑ *Check when completed*

❖ FALL ❖

❧ EVERYDAY TIP ❧

Visit a public garden, or go on a
garden tour. Bring your camera and,
just as important, a notebook.
With or without the help of a guide,
you will find plenty to learn and lots
of inspiration. Be sure to write
down the names of plants or plant
combinations you admire (if there
are no labels, ask someone).

❧ TIP 181 ❧

Cut fragrant flowers early in the day
while they are full of moisture.
Scent resides within the cells of the
petals, so the higher the water
content, the higher the amount of
scent ingredient. Prolong the delight
by displaying them in a vase that is
set in indirect or low light.

☐ *Check when completed*

❧ TIP 182 ❧

Time to start bringing tender and tropical potted plants inside. Give them one last good watering outside, and check thoroughly for insect pests. Groom the plants and cut off all remaining flower stalks and scraggly foliage. Find them a cool, nonfreezing spot, such as a screened-in porch or sunroom.

☐ *Check when completed*

❧ TIP 183 ❧

Plan your fall flowerbeds on paper. Do this as you're checking-out the nursery catalogs. Your plan may be an informal picture on regular or graph paper, but try to make it to scale. Gardening books and nursery catalogs will help you with mature-plant size estimates.

☐ *Check when completed*

❧ TIP 188 ❧

Dethatch your lawn. Thatch is a layer of dead grass that builds up at the soil line, keeping out moisture and nutrients and leading to decline. There are special rakes, as well as power equipment, that can help— but if you don't know what you're doing, hire qualified help.

❏ *Check when completed*

Start favorite vegetables for
the fall garden. Salad and mustard
greens can be sown directly.
Others can be started ahead of time
indoors or purchased as seedlings
down at the garden center—
broccoli, cauliflower, cabbage,
and the like.

☐ *Check when completed*

❧ TIP 190 ❧

Now is a fine time to attend to your bearded iris plants. Pry up the clump with a garden fork. Cut the foliage low; then split it into clumps, each with some fat rhizomes and a little fan of leaves. Replant and water—there's time for the divisions to get established before cold weather arrives.

☐ *Check when completed*

❧ TIP 191 ❧

The flowers of your summer
bulbs may be past their prime, but
be patient with the leaves. Let
them die down naturally. They are
busy sending valuable starches
and sugars into the root system, to
fuel next year's display. Don't cut
off the leaves until they are
completely yellow and limp.

❏ *Check when completed*

❧ TIP 192 ❧

Meadows and wildflower
borders can be cut back or mowed
down now. But do leave the debris
onsite so that it can break down and
return nutrients to the soil. Doing
this also enhances the habitat for
beneficial native insects.

☐ *Check when completed*

❧ TIP 193 ❧

Ripening peppers ought to
be left on the plant as long as
possible. The warm days and cool
nights of fall inspire excellent flavor.
Take only what you need for
tonight's meal. If you are an
impatient harvester, you can bring
some in and let them finish ripening
in a warm kitchen.

☐ *Check when completed*

❧ TIP 194 ❧

Keep an eye on your lawn
and be ready to mow again as
needed. Lawn grass slows
growth in hot spells and resumes
when the weather cools down.
Meanwhile, don't deprive it of
water—but don't overdo either.
Deliver about an inch of water
weekly, until fall rains return.

☐ *Check when completed*

✤ TIP 195 ✤

Now is the time to plant
seedlings of cool-season vegetables.
They relish both organically rich
soil and the cooler fall temperatures.
If you keep them well watered
and feed them (side-dress with an
all-purpose or organic fertilizer),
your cool-season vegetables will be
wonderfully productive.

☐ *Check when completed*

❧ Tip 196 ❧

Tour the yard with a pair
of sharp loppers and good clippers,
now that the summer heat is
dissipating. Take out branches that
are obviously dead, dying, or
damaged—they're not going to
recover. Just this simple operation
helps your plants look much better
and benefits their overall health.

❏ *Check when completed*

Do you feel like your autumn landscape lacks color and punch? Visit a public garden, nursery, or arboretum to find out what is looking fabulous right now in your area. Perhaps you can plant something this year; if not, make a wish list and act on it next spring.

❏ *Check when completed*

❧ TIP 198 ❧

Bring along a shovel and edit your garden—this is an ideal time to remove plants that didn't work out. Perhaps they took up too much space or didn't perform well, or maybe you simply didn't end up liking the way they look. Dig them up and give them away or toss their remains on the compost pile.

☐ *Check when completed*

❦ TIP 199 ❦

Harvest sunflower seeds—
assuming the birds haven't beaten
you to it. Cut the flowerhead off
with about a foot of stem attached
and hang it in a dry, airy location to
finish ripening. Whatever you do,
don't stack or bag the heads, or they
will rot. Ripe seeds can be flicked off
and dried further.

❑ *Check when completed*

❧ TIP 200 ❧

How do you know when to harvest a melon? When it's big? When its skin is colorful? When you thump it and hear a deep thud? If these methods sound too vague, don't worry. Harvest when the stem slips readily from the fruit. Pick it up—if the vine falls away, you are free to walk away with the melon.

☐ *Check when completed*

❧ TIP 201 ❧

Go shopping and treat yourself
to a new pair of gardening gloves!
Try them on first to be sure
they are comfortable and that you
can move your fingers and wrists
easily. If you are really in the mood
to splurge, get calfskin ones—they'll
serve you well for years to come.

☐ *Check when completed*

❧ TIP 202 ❧

Sow a cover crop in any open
spot in need of organic matter.
These annuals germinate in cooler,
moist soil and may even grow some
on milder days. You'll till them
under in a few months. They stop
erosion and prevent nutrients from
leaching away. (What kind? Get
advice from your local garden center
or Extension Service office.)

☐ *Check when completed*

❧ TIP 203 ❧

You may plant lilies now.
True lilies (*Lilium*) settle in well for
next year's growth. A broad selection
of types and colors are waiting for
you down at the garden center. Just
be sure you plant them in good,
well-drained soil in a sunny spot.
They'll bloom in spring.

❑ *Check when completed*

❧ TIP 204 ❧

Sow wildflower and meadow
mixes in prepared soil now for a
sensational show next spring.
Be wary of ones that are not labeled
specifically for your region. Look
out for high grasses content, as this
is basically filler. In any event,
the label should provide basic
planting instructions.

❑ *Check when completed*

❧ TIP 205 ❧

As the air and water temperatures drop, aquatic plants in a garden pond will begin to go dormant. Hardy ones can be cut back and lowered into the deepest water to overwinter; tropical ones should also get a "haircut," but may be safest overwintered inside.

☐ *Check when completed*

❧ TIP 206 ❧

Plant some lavender today!
The plants like plentiful sun and
lean, gravelly soil. Instead of
mulching with compost or bark
chips, which trap moisture
around their crowns, spread pebbles
at their feet. This helps moisture
drain away and keeps your lavender
plants quite happy.

☐ *Check when completed*

❧ TIP 207 ❧

Autumn is a fine time to
lay sod. Get rid of the old grass, as
well as weeds, roots, and rocks. Till
lightly to loosen the soil, sprinkle a
little lawn fertilizer (follow the
amount directions on the bag), and
rake smooth. Put the sod down on a
cool, cloudy day, and water well.

☐ *Check when completed*

❧ TIP 208 ❧

Pick the last tomatoes, especially if frost threatens. Help partially ripe ones continue to turn red by placing them in a bowl with an apple. The ethylene gas that a ripe apple naturally emits hastens this process (no, it's not that the apple is "showing them how it's done"!).

☐ *Check when completed*

❧ TIP 209 ❧

Harvest and cure onions.
While they're still in the ground,
knock over their tops with
a rake. Make your move a week
later—get them out of the
ground, wiped free of dirt, and
arrayed on screens to dry. Only then
can you clip off their tops. Store
in a cool, dry place.

❑ *Check when completed*

❧ TIP 210 ❧

Time to tuck in some color
in the garden gaps. Nurseries and
garden centers will have plenty of
sedums, and ornamental kales and
cabbages for sale. These are
favorites, with good reason. They're
durable and long-lasting, and as
temperatures drop, their color often
gets richer. Mums are also offered in
a rainbow of hues—mix and match!

☐ *Check when completed*

❧ TIP 211 ❧

Cut your dahlias as often as
you can. The more you harvest, the
more the plants will produce—you
can't say that about every flower, but
dahlias never disappoint. Just be
sure you have a tall and sturdy vase
(something tilt-proof!) to hold
them, because some varieties are
quite big and top-heavy.

☐ *Check when completed*

⚜ TIP 212 ⚜

Plant garlic four to six weeks before the ground freezes. Fertile soil is important, but even more important is well drained soil, lest your bulbs rot in soggy ground. (Growing garlic in a raised bed works great.) Plant individual cloves an inch deep, pointed end up, and mulch well. Most of the aboveground growth won't occur till spring.

☐ *Check when completed*

❧ TIP 213 ❧

Find out your area's predicted
first fall frost date. Check your local
paper, or call a garden center or
nearby Cooperative Extension
office. Though it's usually not till
later this month or November,
depending on where you live, you
need to know now so you
can calculate how much gardening
time you have left.

☐ *Check when completed*

❧ TIP 214 ❧

Try raising your own salad mix!
Seed companies call these blends
"mesclun," and they often contain a
range of lettuces, as well as other
tasty edible leafy greens. Sow in
moist, well-drained soil, and lay
down a row cover (it shields them
from a late frost, plant pests, and
hot sun). They grow rapidly.

☐ *Check when completed*

❧ TIP 215 ❧

Plant cool-weather herbs like
parsley and chives. They will grow
quickly in the still-warm soil,
watered in by fall rains, and be ready
to use in a month or two. That's
good timing if you like to use fresh
herbs in holiday cooking or want to
harvest some for gift-giving.

☐ *Check when completed*

✦ TIP 216 ✦

Evaluate your vegetable garden and make notes for next year; tuck these notes where you can refer to them early next spring. Do you need more space for ramblers like squash, zucchini, and pumpkin? Did you have too many tomato plants and not enough peppers? Should the entire garden be bigger or smaller?

❏ *Check when completed*

❧ TIP 217 ❧

Harvest leafy greens. The
flavor tends to be lighter in young
ones and hotter or more intense in
older ones, so make your move
according to your personal taste. In
any event, never cut more than you
can use right away. Flavor and
vitamin levels tend to dissipate in
refrigerated greens.

☐ *Check when completed*

✤ TIP 218 ✤

Plant shrubs or trees. The soil is
still warm, and drenching fall rains
will help water them in. Dig an
ample hole, and mix native soil with
some organic matter for backfilling.
Set the plant in at the level it was
growing in the pot, and press the
dirt firmly around it. Water weekly
until the ground freezes.

❑ *Check when completed*

❧ TIP 219 ❧

Are deer an ongoing problem?
Their destructive dining can be even
more frustrating this time of year,
when they go after young, emerging
plants or ones you've just installed.
Various repellents can work
temporarily, but if those deer are
relentless and you mean business,
you need an 8-foot-tall fence
around your garden.

☐ *Check when completed*

❖ TIP 220 ❖

Bring some herbs in for the winter. Cut them back to live growth first. Then dig them up and put them in pots, watering well. Leave the pots in a sheltered area for a while, checking on them from time to time, just to get them used to container life. Move them indoors into a bright-light location when frost threatens.

☐ *Check when completed*

❧ TIP 221 ❧

Plant cool-season annuals for a
boost of late color. There will be lots
to choose from at the garden centers
right now. Bright selections include
calendula, petunias, and pansies. If
you poke around a bit, you may find
these in new colors or bicolors—
those plant breeders are always busy
trying to dazzle us.

☐ *Check when completed*

❧ TIP 222 ❧

Are your daylilies overcrowded and blooming more sparsely? Divide them now to jumpstart your spring display. Prepare the new bed or area first, though, so the roots don't dry out. Dig up the clumps, and pry them into sections (back-to-back gardening forks might be needed). Replant husky pieces that include a good chunk of roots and some topgrowth.

❑ *Check when completed*

❧ TIP 223 ❧

Plant some peonies! These beautiful, tough perennials relish organically rich soil. The only tricky part is placing them at the proper planting depth—the little pink "eyes" (buds) on their clumping roots should end up no more than 2 inches below the soil surface.

❑ *Check when completed*

❧ TIP 224 ❧

Plant some evergreens—hollies, yews, boxwoods, junipers. Find them at the nursery in large containers or balled and burlapped. Prepare a hole that is deeper and wider than the rootball. Mix in some organic matter with the native soil, and use this improved blend to backfill.

❏ *Check when completed*

❧ TIP 225 ❧

Buying bulbs locally? Examine each
one. It should be clean, with no
blemishes. Squeeze it to be sure it is
firm and plump. Compare it to its
fellows and choose the heftier ones
(light ones are dried up inside).
Note that comparatively bigger ones
have more stored reserves and thus
are more likely to put on a big show.

☐ *Check when completed*

❧ TIP 226 ❧

Plant flower bulbs. Planting
depth varies by type, but the general
rule of thumb is twice as deep as
they are high. If you are digging
individual holes, make them ample
and push some compost into the
bottom of the hole to nurture the
developing roots. Apply fertilizer to
the soil surface afterwards.

☐ *Check when completed*

❧ TIP 227 ❧

Have you admired those random but bright and colorful drifts of spring bulbs, but wondered how to get that spontaneous "naturalized" look? It's easy. Just toss generous handfuls into the chosen area and plant each one where it lands. Dig a hole twice as deep as the bulb's size, sprinkle in some compost, set in the bulb, cover, and water.

❑ *Check when completed*

❖ TIP 228 ❖

Fertilize existing and new bulb plantings with care. If you mix the plant food into the bed, it can burn tender roots at a time when they don't need any stress. Instead, "top-dress" bulbs by sprinkling it on the surface and watering it in. Granular Holland Bulb Booster™ (9-9-6) is great for tulips and other favorites.

☐ *Check when completed*

❧ TIP 229 ❧

To be sure your Christmas cactus blooms on cue, do this. Starting this month, give it dark nights (either move the plant to a dark room or cover it, if it's in a lighted room). Come daytime, a spot in medium light is best. Continue this cycle until plump buds get about a half-inch long.

☐ *Check when completed*

❧ TIP 230 ❧

Feed your trees and shrubs
lightly one last time. At this point in
the year, shoot growth has ceased
and the still actively growing roots
of woody plants will make most
efficient use of the fertilizer's
nutrients. Research has shown that
early spring growth depends heavily
on this stored bounty.

❑ *Check when completed*

❦ TIP 231 ❦

Buy birdseed. The widely
available mixes are not always the
best bet, though. Birds prefer
100 percent sunflower seed, nyjer
seed (thistle), or safflower seed—
these nutritious treats favored by
smaller migrating songbirds.

☐ *Check when completed*

❖ TIP 232 ❖

Start raking fall leaves. If you
wait till they all drop, the job can be
too big! Scoot piles off to one side
or stuff them in paper bags as you
work. You can compost them or use
them as a mulch (chopped up,
preferably—run over them with
the lawn mower).

☐ *Check when completed*

❧ TIP 233 ❧

Renew the organic matter in the tidied-up vegetable garden and now-emptied flowerbeds. Do this before the ground freezes. Well-rotted compost is ideal, or you can buy bagged compost. Dehydrated cow manure and chopped-up fall leaves are also good. Apply it 6 inches deep and dig it in during early spring.

❑ *Check when completed*

❧ TIP 234 ❧

If slugs are always a problem for you, make a pre-emptive strike this fall. Go hunting now for their egg masses in mulch, in your garden soil, in pots, by rotting wood. They're pale yellow and look like little clumps of pearls. Scrape them out with a trowel and destroy them.

☐ *Check when completed*

❦ TIP 235 ❦

Plant perennial types of onions
(bunching onions, shallots).
They don't need special soil or care;
just give them a spot with decent
soil and they'll be fine. Water
them deeply only if rainfall is sparse.
In a few weeks, they'll develop leafy
tops that also happen to be tasty.

☐ *Check when completed*

OCTOBER

✣ TIP 236 ✣

Protect your ripening pumpkins. About now, the skin should be hard and the color should be darkening, but if they are exposed to a light frost, they can turn black—what a disappointment. Just cover the plant with a tarp for the night if the forecast is for cold temperatures.

☐ *Check when completed*

❧ TIP 237 ❧

Should you rake leaves out
from under shrubs and hedges? If
the layer is thick and matted,
or is flush up against the main
stems, yes—it can become
smothering, or harbor pests and
diseases. But a thin layer is okay, as
it will eventually break down and
cycle back into the soil.

☐ *Check when completed*

❖ TIP 238 ❖

Parsley can be saved. You may
already have noticed it is a cold-
tolerant herb. Pick the last green
stems, rinse off the dirt, and dry
with paper towels. Place them into a
plastic baggie, roll the air out,
and seal. The contents will keep in
the freezer for months.

☐ *Check when completed*

⚜ TIP 239 ⚜

Continue to mow the lawn
as long as it is growing. Don't scalp
it, but do keep it looking neat.
This sends it into winter looking as
good as can be expected and means
it will be in better shape next spring
when growth ramps up again.

☐ *Check when completed*

❧ TIP 240 ❧

Make a colorful fall arrangement.
Start with a few branches of vivid
fall foliage. Fill in with softer
textured but bright fall perennials
such as goldenrod and purple asters.
Add a few branches that are adorned
with red berries or red rose hips
(strip foliage from these). Use the
seedheads of ornamental grasses
as dramatic filler.

☐ *Check when completed*

❧ TIP 241 ❧

Rake up the last of the fall
leaves. Don't put larger ones directly
on flowerbeds or the vegetable
garden (even though it's tempting).
They'll only mat down. Run them
through a shredder, or pass over
them with the lawnmower; then
consolidate them in their own pile
(in bags). You'll be able to use
them in 6 months.

☐ *Check when completed*

❖ TIP 242 ❖

Have mushrooms sprouted
in your lawn? They are probably not
a bit harmful, nor can or should
they be killed with a garden
chemical. If their presence bothers
you, or there are a lot of them, your
best bet is to take a rake to
them. Knock off their tops and
cart them away.

☐ *Check when completed*

❖ TIP 243 ❖

Save the seeds that you
scooped out of your Halloween jack-
o-lantern. Spread them out and dry
them on a tray or paper plate, then
put them out for the birds. A
platform bird feeder displays and
holds them well. Cardinals in
particular relish this treat.

❑ *Check when completed*

❧ TIP 244 ❧

Heavy rains begin about now,
and you should plan for them. This
means going through the yard
and creating diversion channels
where needed, so favorite areas
won't get drowned and newly
planted plants won't get dislodged.
A shovel may be overkill; scraping
with a trowel can often do the trick.

❑ *Check when completed*

❖ TIP 245 ❖

Watch for bugs that try to
enter your home or garage looking
for shelter and warmth. Common
culprits include ladybugs. They
won't harm wood, pets, or you, but
they are a nuisance. Your best
bet is to thwart them with caulking
and weather-stripping.

❑ *Check when completed*

❖ TIP 246 ❖

Buy amaryllis bulbs now,
if you want them to be part of your
late-winter or holiday season
décor. They typically take six to
eight weeks to bloom. Get prepotted
"kits," or buy loose bulbs and
pot them yourself. Just remember
that the hefty bulb should be
set half-in, half-out of a well-
draining potting soil mix.

❑ *Check when completed*

❧ TIP 247 ❧

Deal with overhanging or
otherwise risky tree branches now,
before winter comes and wind
or a burden of snow or ice causes
them to fall. Call a tree service
(preferably a certified arborist) to
evaluate your trees for safety.
Get a written estimate, confirm
the service is insured, and
supervise the removal.

❏ *Check when completed*

❧ TIP 248 ❧

Fertilize the lawn. It's much smarter to do this now, rather than in the spring (turf needs fertilizer to get it through the winter). Topgrowth is slowing down or finished, so the nutrients will fortify the roots. Remember to water before and after for the best uptake.

☐ *Check when completed*

❦ TIP 249 ❦

Cut back your taller perennials before frost comes—even if there's some lingering live growth, flowers, or seedheads. Chopping down to within a few inches above the soil level seems brutal, but it will make room for next spring's resurgence. If you want to attract birds, allow the seedheads to remain.

☐ *Check when completed*

❧ TIP 250 ❧

Spare a few perennials whose
dried flowers have winter value.
Birds may enjoy the dried
flowerheads, either as a place to
alight or a seed source. And
whenever snow finally arrives, some
of these plants look beautiful with a
jaunty white cap. Examples include
ornamental grasses, echinacea,
sedum, rudbeckia, and astilbe.

☐ *Check when completed*

❧ TIP 251 ❧

Time to close down the vegetable
garden. Pull out and compost
all plant debris, with the exception
of anything that was diseased.
Mulch with chopped-up fall leaves
or compost (or both), which you
can dig in next spring.

☐ *Check when completed*

❧ TIP 252 ❧

Mulch your perennial beds.
Scoop and shovel on plenty of
mulch, to a depth of several inches
or until the chopped-off crowns of
the plants are out of view. Mulch
protects the roots systems over the
coming cold months, preventing
frost-heaving and moderating soil-
temperature fluctuations.

☐ *Check when completed*

❦ TIP 253 ❦

Plant fresh winter bloomers
like ornamental kale in windowboxes, now. Or, in colder areas,
discard the soil mix, as well as the
dead plants. Scrub out the
windowbox with a brush, and wipe
it down inside and out. It doesn't
take long, and you'll be glad you did
this when spring returns and you
get in the mood to refill it.

❑ *Check when completed*

❧ TIP 254 ❧

Prevent winter weeds by
carefully applying a pre-emergent
herbicide according to label
directions. Make sure you get the
correct product for the sort of weeds
that plague your lawn and garden.
Keep in mind that more is not
better. Rain will water it in.

❏ *Check when completed*

❧ TIP 255 ❧

If you expect the ground to freeze,
dig up gladiolus corms and dahlia
tubers. Dry them on screens for a
day or two, and then clean them off.
Store them in bags in a frost-free
spot. Don't forget to label! And
sprinkle a little fungicide dust into
each bag to prevent rot.

☐ *Check when completed*

❖ TIP 256 ❖

Move emptied pots and containers of all kinds in out of the weather. Rinse them out if they're dirty, and stack them in the garage, shed, or basement to protect from freezing. Instead of getting rid of cracked clay pots, break them into small pieces and save these; they may come in handy for a drainage layer another day.

☐ *Check when completed*

❧ TIP 257 ❧

Brown or rotted spots on your
African violet leaves? This is an easy
problem to solve. It comes from
moisture getting on their fuzzy
surface. That's why the best way to
water these is from the bottom. Just
set the pot in a saucer of water and
let it wick up what it needs.

❏ *Check when completed*

❧ TIP 258 ❧

If your area experiences
windy weather during the winter
months, it can be especially
hard on your (perennial) climbing
plants, including climbing roses. Pay
them a visit and make sure their
major stems are well-attached to
their supports so they don't get
whipped about.

❑ *Check when completed*

❧ TIP 259 ❧

Browse the gardening section in your favorite bookstore. New gardening books are often issued this time of year, just before the holiday season. If you don't buy a title for yourself, at least you can make a "wish list" and place hints for friends and relatives.

☐ *Check when completed*

❧ TIP 260 ❧

Close up the compost pile for the winter. Its activity has been slowing for a while now, and tossing kitchen scraps on it at this point leads only to a pile of chilly or frozen garbage that doesn't break down. Give it one last stir, if possible; then replace the lid or cover it with a tarp to discourage rodents.

☐ *Check when completed*

❦ TIP 261 ❦

Protect marginally hardy rosebushes. The grafted ones, in particular, have a hard time in cold weather and can die down to the rootstock (thus the roses you wanted are killed off). Shovel mulch over the base of the plant, up and over the bulging graft.

☐ *Check when completed*

❦ TIP 262 ❦

Attend a gardening class or an interesting lecture. Flyers for these will be at garden centers, listed in local newspapers, or described in the newsletters of nearby botanic gardens or arboreta. Or poke around on the Internet. It's good to get out of the house—and always worthwhile to get educated and inspired in the off-season.

❑ *Check when completed*

❧ TIP 263 ❧

Indoors, shorter days with less
light inspire spider plants to form
"spiders" at last. Let these grow
to several inches big, then sever
them from the mother plant and pot
up. Nurture them in a warm, bright
room for now; don't neglect
watering. Later, you can move them
into their own hanging basket
or give them away.

☐ *Check when completed*

❧ TIP 264 ❧

Wrap large, tender tub-grown shrubs or trees for the winter. The easiest, most effective way to do this is to create a column of chicken wire all around the pot and twice as tall, at least. Dump in fall leaves. Add a cover, or encase the entire thing in hardware cloth or burlap.

☐ *Check when completed*

❧ TIP 265 ❧

If you haven't already done so, cover the grill and your lawn furniture, if your area receives cold weather for the winter. Or bring them into a protected area inside, such as the garage or basement. If you leave these things exposed to the elements for many months, no matter how durable they are, there's likely to be damage or fading.

❏ *Check when completed*

❧ TIP 266 ❧

Clean your outdoor cushions. Use a stiff brush to get off dirt; then whack out the dust. Put them to dry in a warm area for several days, such as the laundry room (better still, if they will fit, run them through the dryer). There must be absolutely no lingering moisture, or they will get mildewed or smelly in storage.

❑ *Check when completed*

❖ TIP 267 ❖

Move houseplants that spent
the summer outside off the sun porch
or other suddenly chilly area. They
will be better off in a warmer winter
home, such as a windowsill. South-
facing windows are ideal if the plants
are the sorts that need maximum
light. (Remove the screens from these
windows for the winter—it does
increase light slightly.)

☐ *Check when completed*

❖ TIP 268 ❖

Drain the hose and bring it
in for the winter, if your area freezes.
Wipe down its surface with a cloth
so there's no moisture or mud. Don't
hang it. Store it flat, someplace
dry and dark. Let it coil the way it
does naturally; forcing it in
other ways, especially when it is
cold, leads to cracks.

❑ *Check when completed*

❧ TIP 269 ❧

When you're ready to put
them away, clean off caked-on dirt
and mud from shovels and
other large implements. Fill a bucket
with sand and mix in some
vegetable oil until it's moistened.
Plunge in the blade of each dirty
tool. The sand's abrasion will clean
it off and the oil will coat the tool,
which prevents rust.

❏ *Check when completed*

❧ TIP 270 ❧

Save fireplace ashes, assuming you burn regular hardwood logs, not anything with additives. Just scoop them into a bag or bucket and reserve them in a dry place. These can be used in the spring as a soil amendment. They offer potash and lime for your plants.

☐ *Check when completed*

WINTER

❧ EVERYDAY TIP ❧

You don't have to be a Latin
scholar, but it helps to learn the
basics of the scientific plant
naming system. The first word
(italic and always capitalized) is the
genus, and the second word is
the species. If there is another word
set off by single quotation marks,
then that is a specific variety
sometimes called a cultivar.

✣ TIP 271 ✣

Buy some bales of straw
or hay to stockpile for winter
mulching. Straw has fewer weed
seeds than regular hay. Just pile
this off to the side someplace and
raid it as needed in the coming
weeks. It's so much easier to have it
on hand right when you need it!

❏ *Check when completed*

❖ TIP 272 ❖

If someone gives you a plant,
the first thing you should do, sad to
say, is get rid of the colorful foil
or plastic wrapper, which only traps
moisture and can lead to rot.
Once that's off, check that the pot
has a drainage hole in the
bottom. If it doesn't, you are going
to have to repot.

☐ *Check when completed*

❧ TIP 273 ❧

Protect the young trees in your yard from small rodents, including rabbits, that nibble during the winter. If they "girdle" the tree (strip away or destroy bark either part or all the way around), it can die. Thwart these pests by putting a cylinder of hardware cloth around each tree and pressing it into the ground a few inches.

❏ *Check when completed*

❧ TIP 274 ❧

Protect the young trees in
your yard from winter "sunscald,"
literally sunburn that occurs on the
sunny side of the tree during the
winter when it is more exposed.
Wrap the tree with a temporary
bandage of burlap.

☐ *Check when completed*

❧ TIP 275 ❧

Make some durable plant labels,
while you have time and are
thinking of it. Then just stash them
away until next spring. You won't
get everything taken care of, of
course, but you can certainly do
ones for major, favorite plants. Write
on metal markers with grease pencil
or on smooth rocks with a
permanent marker.

☐ *Check when completed*

❧ TIP 276 ❧

Place poinsettia plants wisely, so
they will look good as long as
possible. A windowsill location that
gets six hours of light per day is
ideal. Avoid drafty areas and
temperatures under 70 degrees
Fahrenheit or so. A spot close to a
heat source, however, dries out the
plant and causes the flowers
(actually, colorful bracts) to fade.

❏ *Check when completed*

✤ TIP 277 ✤

You may still be able to harvest
some cold-weather crops out of the
vegetable garden. Root crops in
particular do okay. Indeed, turnips
and carrots seem to be even
sweeter if the weather is cold and
the ground chilly. Just push
aside protective mulch and haul
out what you need.

❏ *Check when completed*

DECEMBER

✦ TIP 278 ✦

A charming holiday gift to give
other gardeners is a decorative
birdhouse. If you have the time and
inclination, you can buy unfinished
wooden ones very inexpensively at
any craft-supply store. Paint them
yourself (or get the kids to do it).

☐ *Check when completed*

❧ TIP 279 ❧

Protect garden concrete—such as pots, urns, and birdbaths—from winter damage. Because it absorbs water that can freeze, concrete cracks all too easily. Waterproof those prized items with a silicon-based water seal, paint meant for outdoor use, or even a thin layer of white cement. At least, empty, cover, and turn over vulnerable pieces.

☐ *Check when completed*

❧ TIP 280 ❧

If deer are a problem in your
area, their browsing inevitably
becomes more intense during the
winter months when sources of
natural food are scarce. You may be
able to discourage them by setting
wire around favorite plants, or even
a blockade of evergreen boughs.

☐ *Check when completed*

❧ TIP 281 ❧

Clean dusty houseplant leaves.
Not only is the coating unattractive,
but it inhibits the exchange of air
and moisture for the plant, which
can be bad for its health. Wipe
them with a soapy sponge, and then
rinse with clear water. Dust and
dirt can be brushed off textured or
fuzzy leaves with a paintbrush or
clean make-up brush.

❑ *Check when completed*

❧ TIP 282 ❧

Check around the perimeter
of the house to find out if plants in
these areas are suffering. Ones
growing under the eaves may dry
out and heave out of frozen or semi-
frozen ground. Ones under
downspouts or clogged gutters may
be deluged. Remedy the situation or
move the beleaguered plants—do
whatever you can.

☐ *Check when completed*

❧ TIP 283 ❧

Make ornaments from pine
or fir cones. Bring them indoors a
few days ahead of time, and set
them in a warm place. This dries
them out completely, evicts
lingering bugs, and ensures that
they are fully open. Roll them in
household glue and dust them with
colorful sequins or glitter. Fashion
loops from ribbons or yarn.

❏ *Check when completed*

❧ TIP 284 ❧

If your yard looks distressingly
barren and colorless this time of
year, resolve to make changes next
year. Go now to area garden centers,
public gardens, or an arboretum and
find out which plants do look nice
in the off-season—and make a note
to see about adding a few when
planting time comes around again.

☐ *Check when completed*

❦ TIP 285 ❦

Prevent small, fragile columnar-shaped conifers from possible winter damage. Winter ice and snow can snap or bend their branches, harming their health and marring their compact look. Just take a long strip of fabric, about 2 inches wide, and wind it around the plant from the bottom to the top, securing the branches.

❑ *Check when completed*

❧ TIP 286 ❧

Make a wreath from evergreen
cuttings from your own yard. Visit a
hobby store and buy a round wire
base, green plastic tape, and green
florist's wire. Press dampened moss
into the base, and wind the tape
around it to hold it in place; make a
wire hook at the top. Poke in the
cuttings thickly all around.

☐ *Check when completed*

❧ TIP 287 ❧

Make evergreen swags for your
holiday décor. Use cuttings from
your yard or the woods; strip their
bases up a few inches. Twist florist's
wire around the bases, and then
attach them along the length of wire
or rope. Using enough greens will
hide the wire from view.

❏ *Check when completed*

❧ TIP 288 ❧

Are you leaving some office
plants on their own while you take
some time off? Make sure they'll
survive your absence. Soak them
well one last time. Then group them
in a bright spot with indirect light
only. Loosely drape a large, clear
plastic bag (such as a dry-cleaning
bag) over them like a tent.

☐ *Check when completed*

❦ TIP 289 ❦

If you travel anywhere with live
plants, protect them. Water them a
few hours before you leave. Just
before you head out, encase them in
newspaper and staple the covering
closed (florists use this method, you
may have noticed). Warm up the car
before putting them in. At your
destination, hurry inside and
unwrap them at once.

❑ *Check when completed*

❖ TIP 290 ❖

Cut Christmas trees fare best if you
recut the base before putting it into
a clean stand or bucket of water.
Various preservatives have been
suggested, including a penny, a
splash of vodka or bleach, and
aspirin. You can try these, but most
important is to remember to top
off often with fresh water.

☐ *Check when completed*

❧ TIP 291 ❧

When wrapping presents,
tuck a sprig of lavender, rosemary,
or other overwintered herb under
the ribbon. Taking the trimmings
won't do the plant any harm this
time of year. And the recipient
will be enchanted with this pretty
and fragrant reminder of summer
days in your garden.

❑ *Check when completed*

❧ TIP 292 ❧

Make some winter potpourri, to
scent the living room or bathroom,
to give away as gifts or to bring
to a hostess of a holiday party. Mix
spruce or fir sprigs, berries, rose
hips, small pine or spruce cones,
seedpods, and dried flowers and
petals. Add cinnamon sticks for
fragrance. Display in small bowls.

❑ *Check when completed*

❧ TIP 293 ❧

Check potted rosemary plants, a popular gift plant this time of year. Because it is technically an evergreen shrub from the Mediterranean, it becomes unhappy in moisture-retentive or soggy soil. You might have to repot yours into a mix that has lots of pumice or perlite, to improve drainage.

❑ *Check when completed*

❖ TIP 294 ❖

Live Christmas trees can
lose needles and dry out in the
warmth of your home. Even the
strings of lights generate a small
amount of heat that adds to the
stress. So keep the plant evenly
moist, and turn off the lights
overnight or when you are out.

☐ *Check when completed*

❦ TIP 295 ❦

Both cut and live evergreen trees
dry out easily in a warm house. For
this reason, you should wait
as long as you can before buying
them, and then keep them cold,
even outdoors, until they come
inside. Spritz them head to toe from
time to time (unless decorations will
be harmed, of course).

☐ *Check when completed*

❖ TIP 296 ❖

Make an unusual, fresh-looking,
and colorful holiday-table
centerpiece this year. Start with a
shallow tray and one or more
colorful pillar candles. Add a thin
layer of water, then fill with
salad greens, cherry tomatoes,
and peppers.

❏ *Check when completed*

⚜ TIP 297 ⚜

Retrieve some of your
homegrown onions or potatoes
from storage, and make a hearty
soup. While you're there, take
a few extra moments to check that
none are rotting or sprouting. If you
find damaged or "iffy" produce,
discard it immediately so the
problem doesn't spread.

❏ *Check when completed*

❧ TIP 298 ❧

Organize your gardening
bookshelf, especially if you receive
more titles as gifts during the
holidays. Separate factual references
from reading-for-pleasure titles.
Group the references by subject, or
by season—whatever makes the
most sense to you. Then, pick one
and put it on your bedside table!

❑ *Check when completed*

❧ TIP 299 ❧

Since light is low this time of year, some of your houseplants might be suffering a bit. If they're developing lanky stems or yellow leaves, or if the entire plant is leaning towards the nearest light source, it's time to intervene and help. Move them, even if temporarily, to a brighter spot—a sunnier, south-facing window or under lights.

❏ *Check when completed*

❧ TIP 300 ❧

Although this is the wettest and
darkest time of the year, one garden
area might still need an occasional
drink of water—it's the space
beneath the eaves of your house!
But look first—don't water there
unless you observe that the area is
dry and plants are suffering.

❑ *Check when completed*

❧ TIP 301 ❧

Organize your garden magazines,
which may be in unread piles. Group
like ones together, in chronological
order, and put them in binders or
cases. Remember that the December
or January issue often contains an
annual index, which you might want
to photocopy and keep separate for
quick and handy reference. Take
your time—stop and read!

❏ *Check when completed*

❖ TIP 302 ❖

Hang a wall calendar for the
coming year, one with big squares
that you can write gardening
notes and ideas onto. Tack it up at
eye level in a high-traffic spot
so you will refer to it often. (Maybe
you received one with a gardening
theme as a gift—if not, they go on
sale about now!)

❏ *Check when completed*

❧ TIP 303 ❧

Planning a big project or installation this year, such as a new patio or terrace, a water garden, or a pergola? It's not too soon to start researching the idea and getting design ideas, from books, magazines, and the Internet. And if you think you will need hired help, line up somebody right now— before his or her calendar fills.

☐ *Check when completed*

❖ TIP 304 ❖

Inventory your seed stash. Some leftovers from last year may still be good, assuming you stored the packets in a dry, cool place. Larger seeds (beans, squash, nasturtium, and morning glory) are more likely to be viable than small seeds (carrots, lettuce, columbine, and poppy). Tiny seeds are less able to retain moisture.

❑ *Check when completed*

✦ TIP 305 ✦

Know before you sow! Slightly dampen paper towels and lay them on a cookie sheet; arrange some old or questionable seeds (about an inch apart). Cover with another damp paper towel, encase the project in a plastic bag, and set in a warm place (at least 65 degrees Fahrenheit). Check back in a few days; ideally at least half should have sprouted.

❑ *Check when completed*

❧ TIP 306 ❧

Time to shop! Gather all
your current seed catalogs. Then
cruise through them with a pack of
yellow sticky notes, flagging pages
with items you want. Compare
similar varieties and look for new
items. Compare prices, check
shipping charges, and make a wish
list. Then pare down the list
to fit your budget.

☐ *Check when completed*

❧ TIP 307 ❧

Order your seeds—for flowers,
as well as vegetables—sooner rather
than later. Mail-order seed
companies get very busy in the next
month or so, and early orders
are fulfilled faster. Plus you are more
likely to get exactly what you want,
with no substitutions or rainchecks.

❑ *Check when completed*

❧ TIP 308 ❧

It's time to stock up on basic seed-starting supplies! You need shallow flats and small pots with drainage holes in the bottoms, labels, several bags of sterile soilless potting mix (available right now at home-supply stores and garden centers), and some plastic wrap for temporary coverings.

☐ *Check when completed*

❧ TIP 309 ❧

Decide where you'd like to keep your developing seedlings, and prepare or clear out the area. Choose a warm area free of drafts. If there is no or poor light, you can provide artificial light. Fluorescent is better than ordinary light bulbs, or you can buy special "grow lights."

❑ *Check when completed*

❦ TIP 310 ❦

Bring more pots of sprouting forced
bulbs from their cold storage into
the house proper. Water them well,
and place them in bright but
indirect light. To help the flowers
last longer, don't display them
anywhere close to a heat source,
particularly not the mantelpiece.

☐ *Check when completed*

❧ TIP 311 ❧

Ornamental grasses may be looking a bit scraggly. Use sharp clippers and chop them down to a few inches above soil level. This "haircut" not only improves their appearance, but also makes way for a fresh flush of growth. Water regularly to nudge them along.

☐ *Check when completed*

❧ TIP 312 ❧

This may be your Year of the Rose!
Check out the All-America Rose
Selections winners; results are
announced in newspaper gardening
columns and winter issues of
gardening magazines (or you can
visit **www.aars.org**). Thumb
through a good book on the topic
by an expert, such as *A Year of Roses*
by Stephen Scanniello.

☐ *Check when completed*

❧ TIP 313 ❧

Order bare-root roses, or buy them
locally. These are dormant plants
and look like a bundle of twigs, but
are actually two-year-old, field-
raised plants that the nursery has
kept in cold storage over the winter.
They often end up being healthier,
huskier plants than the potted ones
you see later in the season.

☐ *Check when completed*

❦ TIP 314 ❦

Impatient? Force branches of
flowering shrubs into early bloom.
This really works, and it's easy and
fun! Cut stems with swelling buds
from forsythia, daphne, willow, pussy
willow, flowering quince, or cornelian
cherry. Split the base up about an
inch to increase water uptake. Then
stand them in lukewarm water and
keep them in a warm room.

☐ *Check when completed*

❧ TIP 315 ❧

Inventory and clean your pot collection. New ones are not cheap, and it's easy to get the old ones back into shape. First, scrape out any residue. Soak very dirty pots in a tub or scrub them with a sponge. Finally, clean everything in a diluted bleach solution (1 part bleach to 10 parts water) and air-dry.

❏ *Check when completed*

❧ TIP 316 ❧

Amaryllis plant all done blooming? Pinch off the fading flowers before the plant expends too much energy trying to go to seed. Move the plant to a sunny window; continue to water it and lightly feed it. The more and healthier leaves it has, the more flower stalks it will be able to generate next winter.

☐ *Check when completed*

❦ TIP 317 ❦

Make a holding or "nursery" area
in a sheltered part of your yard.
Clear it out, define its boundaries
with a low fence or some rocks, and
put in some organic matter. You can
temporarily plant ("heel in") bare-
root shrubs, trees, and rosebushes
here until they are ready to go into
their permanent home.

❏ *Check when completed*

❧ TIP 318 ❧

Review new-plant information
in the gardening magazines. These
annual roundups usually appear
in the January or February issue of
all the major publications and are
great fun to read and dream over.
Here you can learn about a brand-
new disease-resistant rose or a good
new vegetable cultivar.

☐ *Check when completed*

❧ TIP 319 ❧

Icy out there? Unlike snow, ice should not be removed or tampered with, even if the branches of your trees and shrubs are bowing under its weight. You run the risk of snapping the stems. Instead, let the ice melt away naturally. The only exception: If an ice-coated branch is a safety hazard, you should cut it.

☐ *Check when completed*

❧ TIP 320 ❧

Start cool-weather vegetables
such as broccoli and its relatives.
These need time to become
sturdy seedlings so they can be the
first ones out into the garden
when winter is over but before hot
weather arrives (they do poorly
in hot weather). Try to start them
six to eight weeks before you
plan to transplant.

☐ *Check when completed*

❧ TIP 321 ❧

Check on stored vegetables such as onions, garlic, and squash. They should be in a cool, dark place such as the basement or garage. Pull out and discard any that have sprouted, have soft spots, or are starting to rot. They won't be good to eat; plus the problem could spread.

☐ *Check when completed*

❧ TIP 322 ❧

Tune up your hand tools.
With a damp rag, wipe metal
surfaces clean of last year's
encrusted dirt, caked-on sap, or
other crud (or soak or chip it away).
Use coarse sandpaper or steel wool
to sand off rust spots. Finally, wipe
all blades clean with a rag soaked in
linseed oil (or substitute vegetable
oil from your kitchen).

❑ *Check when completed*

❦ TIP 323 ❦

Find out when the last frost is
predicted to occur in your area.
Check your local paper, or call a
garden center or nearby Cooperative
Extension office. It's usually
not till March or April (or even
May), depending on where you live.
This information will help you
plan out the coming weeks.

❑ *Check when completed*

❧ TIP 324 ❧

Sharpen your cutting tools. This means clippers and loppers, of course, but also shovels and hoes. Use a file and restore the original bevel. If the tool is unwieldy, hold it in place with a vise grip while you work. When finished, store the tools in a cool, dry place.

❑ *Check when completed*

❧ TIP 325 ❧

Join a plant society. For modest dues, this is a great way to get information and meet others who share your enthusiasm for a certain type of plant. Benefits may also include regular meetings, plant swaps, plant shows with awards, and helpful publications. To find one, peruse the classified-ads sections of gardening magazines or do an Internet search.

❑ *Check when completed*

❧ TIP 326 ❧

If you haven't done so already,
service the lawn mower. Clean off
the entire surface, above and below.
Then drain the gas, change the oil,
and sharpen the blades before
returning the machine to storage.
You'll be congratulating yourself for
taking the time now, when you
need it to be in top running
condition come spring.

❑ *Check when completed*

❦ TIP 327 ❦

Note weather and garden
events on your calendar or in your
garden journal. Record animal
and bird activity, as well as early
signs of plant life. If you get into
this habit, you'll find the
information really useful in the years
to come, when you are looking for
patterns or want to get an early start
on an outdoor project.

❑ *Check when completed*

❧ TIP 328 ❧

Leftover bulbs—namely, daffodils, tulips, and hyacinths—can go out into the garden, even at this late date, provided the soil is workable (not frozen, not soggy). Mulch afterwards to moderate the effects of fluctuating temperatures. They may or may not bloom this year, but it's better than tossing them out.

☐ *Check when completed*

❖ TIP 329 ❖

Inventory your garden supplies
to see whether you are running low
on anything. Garden stores are
already restocking, and though it
seems a bit premature, there's no
harm in going shopping now to get
what you anticipate needing—
pesticides, herbicides, fertilizers, soil
amendments, stakes, plant labels,
maybe even a nice new tool or two.

☐ *Check when completed*

❧ TIP 330 ❧

This is a fine time to repot your houseplants. They may be potbound, or the soil mix may be compacted or worn out. Your plants will repay you with a fresh surge of growth. Remember to accommodate special needs—African violets like a more peaty mix; succulents prefer extra pumice or perlite for better drainage.

❑ *Check when completed*

❧ TIP 331 ❧

If your orchid plants aren't
blooming, or have inflorescences
with buds that haven't yet opened,
the wait can be excruciating. Nudge
things along by feeding the plants
once a month with orchid fertilizer
(diluted according to the label
directions). Raising the temperature
or humidity may also help,
depending on the type of orchid.

❏ *Check when completed*

❦ TIP 332 ❦

Do your favorite houseplants suddenly have dry edges or brown leaf tips? Low humidity is the culprit, a common problem this time of year. There are several ways to bring them relief: Spritz them occasionally; place them on a tray or dish of pebbles so runoff water can evaporate around them; or place plants closer together.

❏ *Check when completed*

❧ TIP 333 ❧

Prune your rosebushes while they
are still dormant. This is the time to
take out any remaining damaged
canes, as well as crowded and
crossed stems. You may then shorten
the good canes in order to shape
the plant—but never by more than
one-third at any one time.

☐ *Check when completed*

❧ TIP 334 ❧

When your first spring bulbs
pop up, you may greet them with a
light dose of fertilizer to inspire a
good show and general good health
in the future. Wait until they are an
inch or two high, though, and be
sure to follow label instructions so
you don't overdo it.

☐ *Check when completed*

❧ TIP 335 ❧

Some of your bushes and trees, as
well as your roses, may have suckers
emerging from the roots. (Rose
suckers are below the graft.) These
are easier to spot this time of year.
Cut them off cleanly at ground level
with sharp loppers so they never
have a chance to start growing and
stealing energy from the main plant.

❑ *Check when completed*

❧ TIP 336 ❧

Prune your roses. Approach the
project in three main steps: First,
take out all "nonnegotiable" growth
first (dead or diseased wood,
damaged canes); second, thin the
plant by removing rubbing and
crossing branches; finally, shape the
bush by removing small amounts
of growth all around.

❏ *Check when completed*

❧ TIP 337 ❧

Always bottom-water flats and
pots of indoor-raised seeds.
Watering from above is too rough—
the seeds are so small and fragile
that they are easily knocked over or
dislodged. Instead, set their
container in a slightly larger one of
water and let them slurp up the
water they need.

❑ *Check when completed*

❧ Tip 338 ❧

Check out the garden soil.
It may still be too soon to plant
much, but it doesn't hurt to get
acquainted. Scoop up a handful and
squeeze. If the dirt oozes moisture,
it's too soon. If it forms a ball that
breaks apart when poked by your
finger, it's okay to sow early and
cold-tolerant crops (like lettuces,
cabbages, and radishes).

❑ *Check when completed*

❧ TIP 339 ❧

Now is the time to start removing
any winter mulch—compost, straw,
some other organic material,
whatever you laid down last fall—
from your flowerbeds. Wait until the
temperatures are above freezing.
Remove it gradually. Use your
hands, a rake, a leaf blower, or even
some strong blasts from the hose.

❑ *Check when completed*

❧ TIP 340 ❧

If you left some herbaceous
perennial stalks standing over the
winter months to provide
visiting birds with seed or places to
perch, the party is over. Cut them
down to within a few inches of the
ground so the plants can rejuvenate
without obstructing their own
growth. The birds will find plenty
of other food sources now.

❏ *Check when completed*

❧ TIP 341 ❧

As soon as you notice early bulbs like grape hyacinths and crocuses poking up, you may fertilize them to encourage a great performance. Use a fertilizer intended for bulbs, and follow the label directions regarding dosage. Water it in well, unless good soaking rainfall is expected.

❏ *Check when completed*

❧ TIP 342 ❧

Start flower seeds indoors in flats
or pots. Some require light to
germinate and must be laid on the
surface of a flat of seed-starting mix
or sand. Others can be covered
lightly. The seed packet will have
this information. Then place them
in a warm, draft-free spot.

☐ *Check when completed*

❦ TIP 343 ❦

Tuck some colorful annuals in
and among your bulbs. If you do
this while the bulbs are in bloom,
not only does the display look
brighter, but also you won't
inadvertently be digging into the
bulbs or their root systems
like you can when you add flowers
later. Good companions include
pansies and primroses.

❑ *Check when completed*

❧ TIP 344 ❧

When picking daffodils for
bouquets, cut a long piece of stem.
Once inside, though, do some
trimming. There's a pale green or
white section at the very base of
every stem; this should be cut off, as
it won't take up water. One other
thing—pick only a few from each
clump, so you can still enjoy an
outdoor display.

❏ *Check when completed*

❦ TIP 345 ❦

Start a strawberry patch in a sunny site. Since strawberries have shallow roots, the soil should be loose and free of rocks and roots to a depth of several inches. Add a couple of inches of organic matter. When planting, allow each plant about a square foot of space; set the crown just above the soil line.

❑ *Check when completed*

❧ TIP 346 ❧

Pamper a Valentine's bouquet of roses so it will last as long as possible. To do this, prepare a vase of lukewarm water and stir in the preservative powder from the florist. Then recut the stems on an angle (to increase water uptake). Set the arrangement in a cool room overnight to plump up. Then display in a bright room.

❑ *Check when completed*

❧ TIP 347 ❧

Use a cold frame in order to get a jumpstart on the vegetable garden. Right now, you can sow seeds of broccoli, Brussels sprouts, cabbage, and cauliflower. Water well, and wedge some insulating mulch around the pots as insurance. Be sure to close the lid each evening.

❏ *Check when completed*

❧ TIP 348 ❧

Fertilize your shrubs throughout the yard. Use a balanced fertilizer, liquid or powdered, and follow the dilution instructions on the label. It's a good idea to soak the plants, right at their bases, before and after, so the food reaches the roots. (This isn't as necessary if the weather has been rainy.)

❑ *Check when completed*

❧ TIP 349 ❧

Weed with a sharp hoe. It's a quick and easy way to dispatch a crowd of young weeds, which is what you get this time of year. Keep your strokes shallow, though—you don't want to harm the roots of the desirable plants or bring more weed seeds to the surface.

❏ *Check when completed*

❧ TIP 350 ❧

You may now prune your fruit trees, while they are still dormant (that is, before buds show any green). Take out dead and winter-damaged wood, suckers, and branches that rub against one another. Thin the interior so it's not crowded or twiggy. Shape the tree overall.

❑ *Check when completed*

❧ TIP 351 ❧

If you grow ferns, spend a little
time on them now so they will look
their best later. Remove last year's
growth by clipping—not tugging
(or you could yank out the root
system). Cut as low to the ground as
you can, and be careful not to slice
into the new growth that may be
just emerging from the crown.

☐ *Check when completed*

❧ TIP 352 ❧

Repair your lawn chairs! First,
remove the broken or frayed
webbing. Then buy a roll of nylon
webbing at the hardware store—
matching it in terms of width and
color. Cut it to length, weave it
through the existing bands, and fold
the ends to reinforce the pressure
points. Then secure the ends
with snug-fitting screws.

☐ *Check when completed*

❧ TIP 353 ❧

Install edging around beds and
lawn areas. Take a look at the
choices at the home-supply store or
garden center: metal, brick, cedar
shakes, plastic, concrete, and stone.
Whatever you decide, it's a good
idea to dig a trench. This not only
defines your line and holds the
edging, but should help keep
encroaching plants at bay.

☐ *Check when completed*

❖ TIP 354 ❖

Keep a close eye on your fruit trees. As soon as the buds begin to swell, you may spray them with dormant oil. To be effective, the temperature must be over 45 degrees Fahrenheit when applied. This mainly helps to control scale, but it thwarts other pests, as well.

❏ *Check when completed*

❦ TIP 355 ❦

It's easy to plant a small tree or shrub. Dig an ample hole, about 3 times as wide as the rootball but the same depth. Lower the plant into place, check that it is straight and oriented pleasingly, then backfill and tamp the soil down as you go. Water well and mulch.

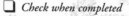 ❑ *Check when completed*

❖ TIP 356 ❖

Evaluate the shape of your
evergreens. If there are branches
jutting out at odd angles, early
spring is a good time to get rid of
them. Don't just shorten them as
much as needed, or you'll be left
looking at an ugly stub. Instead, cut
down low, within the plant, and
no one will be the wiser.

☐ *Check when completed*

❧ TIP 357 ❧

Assuming your deciduous hedge is still dormant, this is the time to cut it back hard if you want to shorten it, rein it in, or reshape it this year. Plants that tolerate such early drastic cutting include privet, laurel, and photinia. When growth does resume, there will be a surge of new young stems.

☐ *Check when completed*

❧ TIP 358 ❧

If weather is wet, your lawn might get an annoying fungal disease known as "red thread." Individual grass blades will be red at first, but brown-tipped as the problem progresses. Unfortunately, there are no good chemical controls. But if you keep the lawn fed, and wait for drier days, it can recover.

☐ *Check when completed*

❦ TIP 359 ❦

A containerized rose can be planted
anytime now. Dig a hole bigger than
the pot and have some extra organic
matter ready to add to it as you
plant. Ease the plant out, and loosen
dense roots with your fingers.
Replant at the same level it was in
the pot, and water well.

❏ *Check when completed*

Expand your resource base by
adding a book to your library.
Cool Springs Press specializes in
state and regional gardening books.
Visit **www.coolspringspress.net**
or check out the list in the
back of this book!

☐ *Check when completed*

❧ APPENDIX ❧

PLANT INVENTORY/HISTORY

name _____

when planted _____

where planted _____

size _____

source _____

price _____

name _____

when planted _____

where planted _____

size _____

source _____

price _____

PLANT INVENTORY/HISTORY

name _____

when planted _____

where planted _____

size _____

source _____

price _____

name _____

when planted _____

where planted _____

size _____

source _____

price _____

PLANT INVENTORY/HISTORY

name _____

when planted _____

where planted _____

size _____

source _____

price _____

name _____

when planted _____

where planted _____

size _____

source _____

price _____

PLANT INVENTORY/HISTORY

name _____

when planted _____

where planted _____

size _____

source _____

price _____

name _____

when planted _____

where planted _____

size _____

source _____

price _____

PLANT INVENTORY/HISTORY

name _____

when planted _____

where planted _____

size _____

source _____

price _____

name _____

when planted _____

where planted _____

size _____

source _____

price _____

PLANT INVENTORY/HISTORY

name _____

when planted _____

where planted _____

size _____

source _____

price _____

name _____

when planted _____

where planted _____

size _____

source _____

price _____

TODAY IN MY GARDEN

TODAY IN MY GARDEN

TODAY IN MY GARDEN

TODAY IN MY GARDEN

My Favorite Sources

MY FAVORITE SOURCES

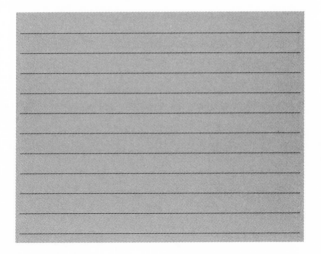

OTHER GREAT BOOKS

FROM COOL SPRINGS PRESS!

Gardener's Guide Series in:	ISBN
California	1-93060-447-5
Rocky Mountains	1-59186-038-5
Washington & Oregon	1-59186-112-8

And that's not all; visit **www.coolspringspress.net** to read about some of our other books!

Managing Editor: Billie Brownell
Cover and Interior Design: Bruce Gore, Gore Studios
Tip Writer: Teri Dunn
Production Design: S.E. Anderson